Children of the Second World War

Memories of evacuation, invasion and imprisonment

HELEN MASSEY

Copyright © 2017 Shauna Massey

All rights reserved.

ISBN 10: 1542868785
ISBN-13:978-1542868785

DEDICATION

Although my mother, Helen Massey, did all the work to compile the stories that are in this book, and is technically the author, sadly she did not live long enough to put it together and complete it. It was a project that she was involved in during the last years of her life and something she was looking forward to producing. So I would like to dedicate this book to its real author, my mother, for being an inspiring role model, a wonderful, gentle person as well as a devoted parent and grandparent.

Shauna Massey

CONTENTS

	Acknowledgements	Pg 1
	Forward	Pg 3
	Introduction: How the Second World War began	Pg 5
1	Outbreak of war and evacuation in Britain	Pg 13
2	Invasion of mainland Europe: Recollections of Scandinavian children	Pg 22
3	War with Britain begins	Pg 32
4	Memories of British children living through the war	Pg 41
5	War-time recollections of German children	Pg 62
6	The Pacific War begins: Evacuation from Hong Kong	Pg 76
7	Conquering colonial territories and capturing prisoners of war	Pg 86
8	Japan surrenders: War ends	Pg 121
	About the author	Pg 127

ACKNOWLEDGMENTS

Thank you to all those who gave their war-time memories to Helen Massey to produce this book. Their stories will live on as an important part of history that should be remembered long into the future.

Christina Anderson
Corinne Bottomley
Birgit Carolin
Peter Carolin
Joan Diamantis
Siri Hoyer Dahl
Michael Fingalson
Joan Franklin
Roswitha Frey
Kensuke Fukae
Konrad Gittinger
Margaret Juett
Patrick Massey
John Monteiro
Mary Norsworthy
David Owers
John Ritchie
Kate Soar
Mary Thomson
Diana Webb
Hannelore Williams
Paul Wong

FORWARD BY SHAUNA MASSEY

Much has been published about the military battles that took place between 1939 and 1945 across the world as two powers – Germany and Japan – attempted to forcefully increase their domination of territories. The far-reaching impact the war had on a generation of children around the world is less well documented. This book is a compilation of memories from people who lived through the war as children in Europe and the Far East. Many were evacuated and became refugees in places that were believed to be safer, while others lived under occupation, often as prisoners, or in hiding. All too often children were separated from one or both of their parents for years.

As some of the stories reveal, although Germany and Japan were the aggressors in the Second World War, innocent children in both countries also suffered terribly.

While life was undoubtedly hard during the war, many of those featured also had some fond memories of that time and some of their stories are funny as well as moving.

This book is a collection of both heart-warming and heart-breaking stories that illustrate some of the experiences children around the world went through during the Second World War. It is important that they be remembered long into the future.

A cutting from The Sydney Morning Herald, announcing the arrival of refugees from Hong Kong to Sydney in 1940. Author of this book, Helen Massey, was one of these child refugees along with her brothers and mother

INTRODUCTION
HOW THE SECOND WORLD WAR BEGAN

A war that engulfs most of the world doesn't happen overnight on the whim of a despot. The treaty that ended the First World War and the settlements that followed caused the turbulence that gave rise to the Second World War. Following is a brief outline of the events that led up to it.

The Armistice that ended the First World War brought peace to the battlefields but not prosperity to the people. Widespread discontent over the Treaty of Versailles grew rapidly after it was signed in 1918. Germany not only lost territory but it had to pay heavy reparations. France felt it was not dealt a fair share of the spoils of war. Italy wanted part of the Tyrol and a chunk of the Dalmatian coast. The Russians weren't even invited to sign the Armistice. Boundary changes meant that thousands of people suddenly found they were living in a different country.

US President Woodrow Wilson initially proposed the establishment of the League of Nations to help keep peace and protect the new borders but ultimately refused to join it. He felt it would drag big nations into every tiny border dispute - and there were signs that there would be many.

Japan was one of the few nations keen to join the League after being promised it could take over German concessions in China. This gave the Japanese control over industries in the province of Shantung - and a gateway into China.

European economies had been seriously disrupted, leaving millions struggling to survive. Food was short, goods were scarce and jobs hard to find. It was against this shambolic background that the seeds of the Second World War were sown.

In 1923 France seized the Ruhr, Germany's industrial heartland, claiming that the Germans had failed to pay their reparations. The German government responded by paying Ruhr workers to walk away from their jobs.

This obliged the government to print trillions of extra marks which, in just a few months, brought the collapse of the currency. The low point came when four billion marks were worth only one US dollar.

Life was also a struggle in Britain. In 1926, tired of poor pay and unsafe working conditions, workers came out in a massive general strike.

The weak economies and governments of Europe had an effect on the United States. In 1929 the American stock market collapsed and overnight rich people became poor. Ordinary people lost their life's savings and it was the beginning of the Great Depression. As businesses collapsed, unemployment soared. Queues of people waited for food handouts and beggars became a common sight on city streets.

With the world in such turmoil, it was not surprising that extreme political organisations began to spring up. Russia was now run by the Bolshevik Communists and many factions and people were inspired by them. Italy's Benito Mussolini was one. In 1919 he formed a small group which was committed to combatting inflation, strikes, unemployment and pillaging of food shops.

A year later he headed a movement of more than 2,000 local groups with over 300,000 members. They adopted an all-black uniform and became known as the Fascists. In 1922 Mussolini became Italy's leader at the age of 39. Three years later he dismissed parliament and became a dictator.

During Mussolini's rise to power, a man in Germany named Adolph Hitler joined a small subversive group called the German Workers Party. Hitler soon found he had a talent for oratory and a gift for organisation. He changed the name of his group to the National Socialistic German Workers - and the Nazi party was born.

Nazis adopted the swastika as their emblem. They greeted each other with raised arm salutes and shouts of "Heil". Dressed in uniforms with brown shirts, dark trousers and high black boots, they called themselves the Storm Troopers.

In 1923 Hitler made his first bid to seize power in Bavaria. He and Herman Goring, with a bodyguard of Storm Troopers, marched into a meeting of local government officials in Bavaria and announced they had taken over the National Government.

Next day Hitler and Goring and 2000 supporters marched into Munich but were quelled by security forces. Hitler was arrested for treason and sentenced to five years in jail where he wrote his book *Mein Kampf*, which became the Nazi bible.

After only nine months, Hitler was released from jail and began contesting parliamentary elections. During this period, Germany's reparations were reduced and bank loans from other countries were paid to Germany, helping it become more prosperous. The election of Paul von Hindenburg as President added stability. However, with the American stock market collapse in 1929, the bank loans started to dry up. The elections of 1930 saw the Nazi party with 107 seats in the Reichstag. Two years later they won 230 seats which, although didn't give them an overall majority, meant they were the biggest party in government.

Hitler forced another election, believing it would give him a majority. In the 1933 elections he gained 288 seats. He proclaimed it a Nazi victory, and asked for an act to be passed giving him the power to rule by decree for the next four years.

The act was passed, but 24 of the Social Democrats who voted against it were subsequently found murdered. Once in power Hitler banned all other parties.

Hitler had an immense flair for promoting his image. He organised spectacular demonstrations where thousands gathered to cheer him and wave Nazi flags. Storm Troopers adopted the goose step as their marching style. Hitler soon found he could work his audience up to a frenzy of Nazi salutes and roars of "Heil Hitler."

At the same time he embarked on a programme of road works to construct the autobahns, the world's first motorways. It was his idea to build a people's car, the Volkswagen, a reliable vehicle the ordinary man could afford.

With all these public works, prosperity returned to Germany. Hitler was admired not only by many of the German people, but also by many of the English aristocracy of the time. The late Duke of Windsor and his wife Wallis Simpson visited Hitler many times and held him in great respect.

Once in power it was not long before the Nazis embarked on systematic persecution of the Jews. They mounted attacks on Jewish shops, homes and businesses and began the wholesale detention of Jews.

At the same time Hitler organised the Hitler Youth movement to brainwash young people into fanatical devotion for Nazi ideals.

Meanwhile Hitler began re-building Germany's armed power. In 1936 he moved troops into the Rhineland, an action that violated the Versailles peace treaty. France protested to the League of Nations, but they were already regarded as powerless.

The previous year he had introduced conscription of young men into military forces and formed a new air force, the Luftwaffe.

Hitler planned to extend the boundaries of Germany to incorporate Austria, which was largely sympathetic to the Nazis, and Czechoslovakia, which would give more strategic boundaries to his Greater Germany. This was all part of Hitler's plan laid out in his book, *Mein Kampf*.

Whatever worries other European countries had about Hitler's rising strength and aggression were washed aside as they were all too embroiled in their own economic difficulties to be concerned.

Hitler marched into Austria in March 1938, with the approval of Mussolini and a rapturous welcome by the Austrians.

Next he turned his attention to Czechoslovakia, which had a very large population of Sudetan Germans. They strongly supported the Nazis and wanted to become a German state within Czechoslovakia. Britain and France, determined to avoid war, urged the Czech government to cede to Germany all areas where Sudetan Germans were in the majority. Feeling betrayed by their allies and seeing no alternatives, the Czechs conceded.

Britain's prime minister, Neville Chamberlain, then signed a peace pact with Hitler that allowed him to build up his naval power up to one third of Britain's navy. Although it was known Hitler had been building warships and submarines for years, Chamberlain thought this would restrict the size of his naval strength.

Chamberlain returned to London, elated at his achievement, and declared that for Britain it meant "peace in our time".

In fact it spelled doom for Czechoslovakia. Hitler soon afterwards announced he wanted the rest of Czechoslovakia as well, a demand that was meekly conceded by Britain and France.

Hitler's next project was to recover Danzig. Formerly a German port on the Baltic, it was given to Poland, along with a corridor of territory, by the Treaty of Versailles so that Poland could have a route to the sea. The Polish foreign minister, Joseph Beck, was struggling to find a way to keep Russia, on its eastern border and Germany on the west, at arm's length.

Chamberlain, believing Poland was in no danger, offered, along with the French, to guarantee Poland's security. Russia and Germany then signed a mutual non-aggression pact. This freed the Soviets to make whatever moves they wanted against countries along their border, such as Finland, Estonia and Latvia. And without the threat of Soviet intervention, it opened the door for Germany to attack Poland which it did just one week later, on September 1.

Two days later France and Britain declared war on Germany.

****

CHAPTER ONE
OUTBREAK OF WAR AND EVACUATION IN BRITAIN

Before the outbreak of war, during a decade of debate, the British government decided that in the event of war, whole cities could not be evacuated along with their industries. So a programme was drawn up for the evacuation of schools.

The Women's Voluntary Service (WVS) was formed to investigate rural areas that could take evacuees and helped carry out house-to-house surveys to identify who had space to take in refugees. Large mansions were often requisitioned for schools.

Authorities in Britain were well aware that the bombs dropped on London in World War One showed that the island nation could not rely on the English Channel to keep back invaders, as it had ever since the 1066 Norman conquest.

When evacuations began, the WVS was mainly responsible for arranging assembly points, organising trains, buses and even boats to carry the children. Rehearsals were carried out - children were assembled and marched or bussed to the train stations.

Each child was given a number and had a label with their name sewn or tied on to their clothes. They were allowed to take one suitcase and were given a list of items they should take, which included a gas mask and a packed meal for the journey. Each child was allowed to take only one toy.

Mothers had to say goodbye to their offspring not knowing at what address they would end up at. Some didn't even know the destination. Whole trainloads of children had to be worked into the normal rail timetable to avoid upsetting schedules. At their final destinations, children were usually herded into a hall and local people, who had been told they were to take in refugees, made their selection.

Mary Thomson was among the first to be evacuated from London and recalls a very unhappy experience:

I think it must have been the first time I ever spent more than a day without my family and there I was, aged eleven, marching away from school in a straggling line, clutching a little suitcase and my gas mask.

I'd no idea where I was going that day in late August 1939, or whether I'd ever see my home again. Mother didn't know I was gone. She was out delivering leaflets to people in the streets explaining the mass evacuation of London children.

After quite a long walk we were ushered on to a train by our teachers. It was my first ever train journey, unbelievably. Dad was a motor trader, and we were the only family in the road with a car. (I'm not showing off - you fell out if you leaned on the doors and the brakes screamed like a banshee. This was particularly embarrassing in front of my car-less schoolmates.)

We ended up, bewildered, in a small country village only about 20 miles from London. We were not the only bewildered people. Our hosts had been told to expect a small group of teenage boys. They showed their disappointment. We were left forlornly standing in the village hall - trying to look like desirable adoptees. It didn't work for me. A girl in my class, whom I didn't know very well, had joined me, with her two younger brothers.

It became clear very quickly that there weren't going to be many volunteers to take in a group of four London kids.

Some hours later we were still standing there, hungry, having demolished the welcoming present of a minute chocolate bar, after all the others had been chosen and escorted out of the hall. Eventually the organisers returned. The good news, they told us, was that they had found us a place. The bad news, which they didn't tell us, was that it was the only genuine prehistoric rural slum in the otherwise prosperous neighbourhood.

The first thing we asked for, on being handed over to our hosts, was to visit the bathroom. Mysteriously, they pointed out to the garden. Out we trotted in an anxious line of four. We weren't mystified for long. Our noses led us to a ramshackle hut. Inside was a rough wooden seat holding a bucket, which had been liberally used, and not recently emptied. We all cried. In fact, we cried for a week. The authorities gave in. They had, they said, found us something nicer, but we'd need to be on our best behaviour.

Neither of these statements was an exaggeration. We went from the depths to the heights. We had been allocated to the local manor house, with its sweeping drive and tennis courts. The owner had previously refused to accept any London urchins. He was a complete relic – an elderly, ex-army officer of the old school. They had appealed to his sense of duty, I suppose. As soon as we were delivered to him we were assembled and addressed by the colonel. He expected us, he said, to act like true English men and women, to remember our duty to King and Country, and to be brave.

This left our group of four, whose combined ages would have hardly added up to one mature patriotic citizen, somewhat baffled. We were not left in the dark too long about our status. We were to have a servant to look after us. We were neither to be seen nor heard in the main house, and would only speak when spoken to by the colonel or his elderly lady. We were to eat in the kitchen. Quietly. As the only alternative was probably a return to the dreaded outdoor lavatory we agreed. Or did they even ask us? I doubt it.

And so for weeks we lived a life far removed from the London suburbs, worried about the safety of our parents left behind in a London that might at any moment be bombed like Warsaw. But we behaved. However, *one of us accidentally knocked over a small fence. But, even in the face of the colonel's exhortation to own up, none of us told tales or confessed. (It was me who knocked it over – riding on a borrowed bike.)*

Soon it emerged that our school had been sent to the wrong place, and we were moved to a town a few miles away. Before we left the manor house, we plotted how to break into the main house, to slide down the forbidden oak bannister and knock down and jump on one of his treasured suits of armour, just to outrage the colonel. We chickened out and left, thanking him for having us, just like our mothers had taught us to do.

In the new place everything was well organised. All our places were decided in advance.

Once again I drew the short straw. The two brothers went next door and settled happily with a family with children. My friend Pat and I were placed in a small house on a grubby estate with hosts who were, to put it mildly, not suitable – Mr. M. was a gloomy depressive and Mrs. M was frankly weird, verging on being a total nutcase.

Once again we cried, but this time it didn't work. We stayed. I cried all day when my mother visited me. Next week she came again. For her sake I decided to be brave. I only found out much later that she had come to take me home. She mistook my bravery for acceptance. I abandoned the stiff upper lip policy after that which nearly cost me my life as I became very ill, and was in dreadful pain. Mrs M told me not to make a fuss. In the end, urged by neighbours, she finally called a doctor. I was rushed to hospital with peritonitis and operated on immediately. After I'd spent a month in hospital, my parents took me home. I arrived just in time for the start of the aerial blitzkreig on London. But after evacuation, it was nevertheless still a great relief to be home.

·········

Patrick Massey and his younger brother Mick were also evacuated from London with their school to Bexhill-on-Sea, a resort town on the South Coast of England facing the English Channel. This is how he recalls the outbreak of war.

The man on the wireless said war with Germany had just started and sure enough, not two hours later, the air raid sirens went off. I stared at the sky above Bexhill-on-Sea half hoping, as an 11-year-old boy would, to see dogfights and dive bombers like the ones in those Errol Flynn movies. But alas, all we saw was a flock of swallows hurrying south to safer climes. When the birds dipped over the horizon the all-clear sounded.

Bexhill on Sea in Sussex had been selected by authorities as a safe haven to which we could be evacuated from our school at Blackheath in south London. By late August, 1939, everybody knew war was coming. So two days before it began they packed us off on trains with our gas masks in square cardboard boxes and large labels attached to our collars.

Nobody, least of all the Imperial General Staff, imagined that within 12 months France would have collapsed and that Hitler's panzer divisions would be parked on the French coast only 50 miles away from Bexhill. What's more they showed every intention of crossing the water to visit this genteel Sussex resort. But in those late months of 1939 there was little to disturb the calm.

My brother was billeted separately with boys of his own age while I and a classmate called Peter Murray were lodged at the house of three middle-aged spinsters who felt duty-bound to help the war effort. In those days, middle-aged spinsters were much in evidence because the men they might have married 20 years before had failed to make it back from the trenches of World War One. The presence of two small boys in this prim household proved something of a strain to the ladies living there.

They insisted on scrubbing us vigorously in the bathtub every evening, ignoring our pleas that at home, bath nights came only on Wednesdays and Fridays. "It's all right, we're used to seeing little boys," one of them said, rather puzzlingly I thought.

We tried to show appreciation. One day we took home a catch of specially plump shrimps netted on the beach and offered them up to be cooked for tea. The ladies ate them decorously but with every sign of enjoyment. "And whereabouts did you catch these?" one of them beamed. My classmate told her it was in a pool under that big pipe which led into the sea. The spinsters looked aghast and never again treated us with quite the same benevolent tolerance.

By the end of the year it had remained so quiet in London that our parents brought my brother and I back home. On our last night with the spinsters I asked if they would be taking in any more evacuees. They stared silently at the ceiling.

A young Patrick Massey (left) guarding the shores

****

CHAPTER TWO
INVASIONS OF MAINLAND EUROPE: RECOLLECTIONS OF SCANDINAVIAN CHILDREN

Although war had been declared between Germany and Britain, Germany was as yet far too busy to attack territories in Britain or France. First, Hitler hurled the bulk of Germany's new-found military might against Poland. Luftwaffe aircraft dropped thousands of bombs on the cities. At sea their navy battered Danzig. On land masses of tanks and artillery poured across the country.

The Poles fought back bravely with obsolete and inadequate equipment. At one point Polish cavalry, armed only with lances and swords, charged advancing lines of tanks. It was a bloodbath. Hitler had counted on the French not to support Poland, and they did not fail him. Within days Poland was defeated.

The period of quiet in Britain after the declaration of war became known as 'the phony war'. It gave Britain a chance to strengthen its forces and manufacture planes, guns and ships.

Winston Churchill was then First Lord of the Admiralty. He realised that much of the steel Hitler needed for his armaments came from the northern mines of Norway, and were shipped out from the port of Narvik. His plan was to mine the coastal waters of Norway to prevent the

German ships getting through.

Hitler had already realised the importance of dominating the North Sea, not only to allow his cargo to be transported safely, but to use as a base for attacking British ships leaving their ports in the north of England and Scotland. He planned to seize every port and airfield in Norway. A reconnaissance plane spotted the German fleet heading north and British warships were sent out to find them but fog and bad weather prevented the Navy from finding the German fleet and it slipped through into Norwegian ports. On land the German troops had conquered Denmark in just a few hours. Aircraft loaded with infantry then landed in Oslo, Norway.

Siri Hoyer Dahl was living in a coastal town of Norway and recalls the invasion.

On the morning of April 9th, 1940, my mother woke us up weeping: "Our country is at war!" I had never seen a tear on my mother's face before. Grown-ups did not cry. Nothing much happened that day. My father, though, marched up and down the road as far as the hospital fence went.

I grew up in a small town on the western coast of Norway called Molde. Before the war there were about 4,000 people there. We lived in Molde from 1936 to 1946. It was known as The Town of Roses because practically all the houses, including the ones in the main road, had little gardens with roses growing. My father was a doctor specialising in tuberculosis and was head of a sanatorium for approximately 150 patients. Shortly before the outbreak of war, he'd spent a year studying in Berlin, so he was prepared for what was to come. During the winter of 1939 my mother had been knitting socks and balaclava helmets for soldiers fighting in the war in Finland.

The day after the war was announced, it was arranged that my 10-year-old sister, Berit, and I should take a bus and stay with family friends an hour's drive away from town. The bus stop was by the dock. We put our luggage inside the bus. Then the air raid warning chased us into the basement of a nearby hotel. Hundreds of people were there. The building shook and the lights went out. I was surprised that the grown-ups seemed to be afraid. That had never happened before.

When we finally got out there was a bomb crater beside the bus, and the bus itself was not in a condition to drive. But our satchels were okay. Then the towns-people started fleeing in panic. In slippers and aprons, the housewives came running out of their houses. We ran with all the others, along the roads leading from town and some went up into the forest. After a while we were offered a lift in a lorry, which brought us most of the way to our friends in the country. The Germans had only dropped a few bombs that day and no houses were hit. But in the fields there were deep holes that rapidly filled up with water. Seeing as there was no more bombing, a week later our parents came to bring us home.

When I returned, the basement windows of our house were covered with sandbags and the basement was filled up with hospital beds with heavy quilts for the family and others to sleep in. One night, two British officers and a boy who looked about 15 were there too. The boy was a gunner on one of the British boats out on the Romsdalsfjord. He had not been quick enough in removing his hand from the cannon's mouth and had lost two fingers. I can still hear him weeping.

When we returned, the main street of our Town of Roses was changed into two rows of black chimneys. The wooden houses were gone. Ours was not. It was situated in a big hospital park, which saved it. My parents stayed there, keeping watch over the old hospital building, while the patients were evacuated to a school a mile west of the town.

We children were given beds in a friend's house, a short walk from town. We were allowed to go home for a few hours on quiet days.

One day it took me more than an hour to get home as I had been "playing war", bombing my bark boats with stones in the water-filled shell holes along the path. My frightened mother came looking for me. Then one night the bombers returned and hit the tuberculosis sanatorium, in spite of a big red cross painted on the roof. My father had recently obtained x-ray equipment and was eager not to lose this. So my parents raced over into the burning old wooden building and managed to drag the heavy thing down one flight of stairs. Suddenly two British officers were there at their sides helping them to get it out. Having done so, they disappeared.

After this the Germans arrived and took over the town. They lived in our school and marched in the streets singing "Denn wir fahren gegen Engeland" ("Now we shall go and take England next").

The hospital was re-established in a remaining house for children close by. Walls and roofs were put up over the old basements to serve as kitchen and dining room for the staff. To a seven-year-old child it felt like a positive thing, this building activity, and it was hard to understand that the nice young carpenters were working for the Germans and should not be spoken to. We were not allowed to receive sweets from the soldiers, and would immediately tell on those who did.

As the school building was occupied, we were taught in a clothes factory. Food was rationed, but with farmland and a fishery close by there was no real need. Besides, we had 'Swedish soup' a pint of pea soup or oat soup per child per school day that we were allowed to bring home and add to the family dinner. The population of the town halved to 2000, in spite of Swedish Aid, which gave many families a new home.

One winter's day - I must have been around nine - I had an accident with my sledge, which was not all that easy to control. The road down by the river was steep and I crashed into a German officer's black leather boots from behind. He fell and he was bleeding from his left ear. I was shivering with fear for what I had done. We were at war and he was an enemy that I had harmed. I was so anxious that the family might be punished I cried myself to sleep for many a night.

Our father was a leading member of a civil protest organisation called Home Front. All the members used aliases to protect their identities. One of the members who knew the real names of all the members was arrested by the Germans, which made my father very tense until the end of the war.

....

Reknes sanatorium 1940

Siri Hoyer Dahl (third from left) with her family in Molde, Norway in 1940 after they had returned from evacuation.

Hitler had now conquered Denmark and Norway and Sweden became neutral. Germany and the Soviet Union were at peace with each other, having recently signed a treaty of mutual non-aggression. Yet Moscow knew that it would not be long before Hitler's forces invaded the USSR. What worried the Soviet government was the position of the Finnish border, which at one point lay only 20 miles from Leningrad. If the Germans invaded through Finland (which they eventually did), Nazi forces would quickly find themselves within artillery range of the city.

As early as 18 months before World War Two began, the Russians had embarked on negotiations with Finland to reduce this threat. What they mainly wanted was to control the Karelian Isthmus and thereby push the border back a good 100 miles from Leningrad. Helsinki declined and on November 30, 1939, the Red Army invaded Finland in what they thought would be a war lasting no longer than a week. In fact it took more than three months before the Finns were subdued. They showed astonishing powers of holding back the overwhelmingly superior Soviet forces with guerrilla tactics in which tanks were destroyed by petrol bombs. Peace between the two countries would not be made until the Paris Peace Treaties were signed after the war in 1947.

As a child in Finland, Christina Anderson remembers those days:

Children of the Second World War

I was four or five years old when war broke out between Finland and Russia. However, my memories of the Russian occupation are from around the age of seven to ten. My father had been called up as a soldier to fight in the trenches. I remember him coming home on leave without teeth, and I wondered what the Russians wanted them for. I presumed that they'd been extracted due to his poor diet.

Before the war started, my father was the manager of a large country estate, Soderlangvik near Dragsfjard, Kimito, in southwest Finland. Because all the men of fighting age were called up, my mother (who was then 32) was left in charge of the estate. I have patchy memories. I remember my little brother being born as the bombs were falling and exploding. And when my sister and I went to school in the snow we had to wear white overalls so that we could lie in the snow when the alarms sounded and not be seen.

On the estate, we had Russian soldiers as prisoners, not in cells but working freely about the place. They must have been like any other fathers missing their children for they were so gentle and tender to us. My memories are of them singing, with soft voices, beautiful Russian lullabies, and making small wooden toys for us like dolls' beds and small wagons.

I remember the term 'black market' being mentioned a lot, usually after we received things like sweets, clothing and other things you could not buy in the shops. I always wondered why it was called 'black' as it produced such good bounty.

Once my sister and I were given name tags as we were to be evacuated to Sweden, which was a neutral country. However my mother took our tags off. She apparently changed her mind at the last minute about evacuating us. My baby brother spent his first year in the bathtub! It was the only room with no windows and it was the best place to protect us from the shrapnel of bombs.

I was not a bad little girl, but when my sister was saying her prayers at night she asked God to bless everyone, including Molotov, a Russian leader. However, I prayed that my father would shoot him with his gun!

I remember once being so frightened that I vomited in the hall. Mother always reassured me that everything would be fine and that I would grow up and get married. I remember then thinking that the bombs will not kill me now, as the war will most likely be over when I get old enough to marry. I felt much happier then.

****

CHAPTER THREE
WAR WITH BRITAIN BEGINS

Within a day of war being declared, a German submarine, without warning, torpedoed the British passenger liner *Athenia* resulting in the loss of 112 lives. Although on land war had not yet touched Britain, it was a different matter at sea. Germany had built up a large fleet of submarines and the head of its navy, Commodore Donitz, realised the best way to defeat the British Royal Navy and to win command of the seas was to unleash his submarines.

In October Donitz sent a single U47 submarine into Scapa Flow, in Scotland's Orkney Islands. This was the British Home Fleet base, and silently, in the middle of the night, the U-boat navigated its way through the channels and attacked the battleship Royal Oak. It scored a hit and the submarine turned to escape. When the commander of the U-boat realised the battleship had not been sunk, and there appeared to be no sign of retaliation, he turned and made a second attack. This time he sank the battleship and 833 mariners aboard lost their lives.

Following their triumph, the German Navy was ordered to sink all British and French merchant ships, which were unarmed, without warning. The German fleet lost no opportunity to attack every ship they could find. Hitler reasoned that without the vital life-line of ships to supply raw materials, food, arms and troops, Britain would soon surrender.

In London Neville Chamberlain was swept out of power and Winston Churchill became prime minister. Hitler was preparing to control the shores of Europe in preparation for his invasion of Britain. Finland was under attack by the Russians. The British had planned to send a force to help repel them but with the outbreak of war they were unable to help. The Finns were forced to surrender and cede territory to the Russians. With Norway and Denmark already under his control and Sweden remaining neutral, Hitler's next targets were Belgium and Holland.

Hitler's ultimate target was to take the north of France. The French prepared to defend their country and mobilised five million men to man their Western Front - the Maginot Line. German troops kept them occupied and pinned down with sporadic attacks. The British had already sent four divisions to France to blockade ports in an attempt to stop supplies reaching Germany.

Suddenly at dawn on May 10, 1940, a wave of tanks and infantry broke across the borders of Belgium, Luxembourg and Holland. Parachute troops were dropped behind the Dutch lines to capture roads and bridges.

The Dutch fought fiercely, and kept control of key bridges to hold back the Germans. They hoped the Allies would come to their rescue. But the British had planned to stop the Germans at Belgium leaving only the French to advance to southern Holland. The German air force bombed the Dutch capital, the Hague, and within two weeks Germany was in control of the three countries.

The French were pushed back to the south of France and the British Expeditionary Force were ordered to retreat to Dunkirk. The British commander, General Gort, felt getting the troops to Dunkirk would be the only hope of getting them back to England. What he did not know was that the German troops were closer to Dunkirk than the British. Fortunately Hitler had ordered his panzers to stop 12 miles north of Dunkirk.

The British, along with what was left of the French troops, were strafed by German dive bombers and artillery. The British navy was busy in the Atlantic and had few ships they could send in close to the shore. Thousands of small craft were commandeered in England - fishing boats, river barges, pleasure boats, even paddle wheel steamers - crossed the Channel time and time again to rescue troops from the beaches. As ships were sunk, the harbour became clogged with wrecks, but still the small boats came in. Nearly nine hundred boats, under constant attack, brought back over 200,000 British troops and over 100,000 French.

Hitler had conquered mainland Europe and now it wanted Britain. With his commanders, Hitler stood on the shores of France and gazed across the Channel to the white cliffs of Dover. His generals wanted to attack as soon as possible but Hitler ordered them to wait. He believed that with Britain standing alone, losing control of the seas and the supplies that they so desperately needed, they would surrender. His contacts with some of the aristocracy led Hitler to believe they would welcome a peace treaty. Churchill seemed to encourage such overtures. But he was really playing for time.

Britain was totally unprepared for war. After the First World War, few attempts had been made to build up any of the Forces. The once proud Navy Fleet was largely outdated. The Air Force had been totally neglected and now, after Dunkirk, the Army was in complete disarray.

But since declaring war on September 3, 1939, time had not been wasted in Britain. New tanks had been built, warships were being constructed, and most importantly, the latest fighter aircraft, the Spitfire, was being churned out as fast as possible. Coastal defences were put in place and men were conscripted into the Forces.

The delay Hitler imposed on his generals gave Britain time to prepare for the assault that was inevitable.

In the meantime German forces swiftly finished off the French. Their well-equipped and stronger forces were too much for them. The 'invincible' Maginot Line collapsed with little opposition and Hitler's troops marched unopposed into Paris on June 14. About a week later France surrendered. The Germans occupied and controlled the northern half of France and the Atlantic coastal areas. Below that, up to the Mediterranean Sea, the Germans installed the Frenchman Marshal Petain to govern the rest of France but in collaboration with Germany.

Finally, in July, without a country in Europe to oppose him, Hitler made plans to invade Britain. His plan was first to launch 'Operation Sea Lion' which was to attack British Naval Bases and shipping.

The Luftwaffe, the German Air Force, not only outnumbered British airplanes, but their pilots had battle experience from the Spanish civil war. The British Spitfires took heavy losses by flying in tight formations, which gave them no room to manoeuvre.

When Hitler launched phase 2, 'Operation Eagle Attack', his plan was to destroy RAF bases, airfields, aircraft factories and defences which, he reckoned, would leave the way clear for phase 3, the invasion of Britain.

Germany's Operation Eagle Attack became UK's Battle of Britain. In mid August the Luftwaffe sent out waves of bombers with fighter escorts to destroy aircraft on the ground, bomb airfields and ports. British pilots stayed on the alert, taking off as soon as radar picked up the squadrons heading their way. The Germans were constantly amazed how the British always seemed to know when they were coming. Although they had heard talk of a secret weapon called radar, they did not place much credence on it.

Day after day, German planes left their airfields across the channel to inflict as much damage as they could on the British. The British pilots were less experienced than the Germans but, swiftly, the Spitfire pilots developed tactics by flying in smaller groups. The new Spitfire was much faster than the German Messerschmitts and it could inflict considerable damage on the slow-flying bombers.

Britain was short of pilots and newly trained young men were sent into combat with very little flying experience. As wave after wave of German bombers were filling the sky over southern England, British pilots were exhausted, airfields became so damaged many were out of action, and enormous numbers of fighters had been destroyed. Air Chief Marshall Hugh Dowding felt defeat was near. Only a miracle, he believed, could save Britain now. And miracles can happen in the most mysterious ways. The Luftwaffe had followed Hitler's orders not to bomb London - only strategic targets such as airfields, ports, shipyards, factories constructing airplanes, munitions and any other targets directly implicated in the war. Cities, with their civilian populations, were not to be targets, he ordered.

One night a couple of German bombers out to attack factories and oil storage tanks south of London, got lost. They jettisoned their bombs and retreated from the fierce flak surrounding them. At that time they were flying over central London. The bombs killed people coming out of cinemas or pubs or on their way home.

Churchill immediately retaliated. He instructed RAF bomber aircraft to bomb Berlin. Although they did not cause much damage, it meant the war had entered a new phase. Three more strikes over Berlin embarrassed Goring, who had assured the German people that no enemy bomber would ever reach Berlin.

Hitler was furious. He ordered massive retaliation. Hundreds of Luftwaffe bombers flying high and protected by fighter aircraft flew unimpeded over London. Anti-aircraft fire from the ground was unable to reach their height and with little trouble the Luftwaffe dropped thousands of tons of bombs over the east end of London. Soon the sky was red with blazes from shipyards, factories, docks and homes. Hundreds of people were killed and thousands injured.

Hitler had promised he would drop a hundred bombs on London for every bomb that had fallen in Berlin. For the next week, bombers flew round the clock bombing London. Thousands more were killed and ten thousand injured. But by bombing London the south coast airfields were speedily being repaired, fighters made airworthy and pilots replaced and refreshed. Fighter Command began to attack bombers and their escorts in the air.

September 15 was to be the day Hitler would invade England. Goring thought that the RAF had been destroyed and that the heavy bombing would ease the way for ground troops to march in. As soon as German aircraft reached Britain's shores, radar signals giving their positions went out to the waiting fighters. Every British plane and pilot available was ready to fight them back. Many German escort fighters ran out of fuel and had to turn back or they crash-landed. Hitler's Operation Sea Lion, his invasion day, became the Battle of Britain.

As his aircraft limped back, Hitler realised that the war with Britain would be a long one. They would not surrender in days or weeks like the rest of Europe.

He did not know how close to defeat Britain was. Every aircraft they possessed, and every pilot available, had been sent up in a last-ditch stand to repel the Germans. The Battle for Britain had been won. But war was not over.

****

CHAPTER FOUR
MEMORIES OF BRITISH CHILDREN LIVING THROUGH THE WAR

Many of the children who had been evacuated to rural areas during the Phoney War had returned home to London and the surrounding areas because there was no bombing. So when the Germans did start to bomb civilian areas in Britain, they experienced the full force of it.

Patrick Massey recalls his experience following his return to Catford in south east London from evacuation in Bexhill:

London remained peaceful until the summer when the Battle of Britain began. Then we really did see those dogfights and dive bombers all over the sky. We cheered wildly whenever a plane plummeted down with smoke streaming from its tail - on the questionable assumption that it must have been German.

The Battle of Britain ended in Britain's favour with the RAF still largely intact. But then the Blitz began. Every night the sirens sounded and we retreated to the end of the garden to settle in our Anderson shelter, a corrugated iron structure covered in two feet of densely packed earth. From here we listened to the distinctive throb-throb of German heavy bombers and the deafening blast of anti-aircraft fire. At frequent intervals we heard the frightening whoosh and whistle of a descending bomb.

Peeping outside the shelter we saw searchlights blazing and the red bursts of ack-ack shells. Rarely were the bombers hit and in those days fighter planes didn't work well at night. Nearby houses were flattened and some neighbours killed. Our home escaped with just fallen ceilings and broken windows. On my morning paper round I frequently had to wheel my bike around craters in the road. Aged 12 by this time, I felt more excitement than the fear I would have experienced as an adult.

One of the great pastimes in those days was collecting shrapnel fallen from exploding anti-aircraft shells. The competition was to see who could find the largest lumps of splintered metal. I couldn't help reflecting that the jagged projectile in my hand had been intended to knock holes in an enemy aircraft and perhaps its crew.

After a few months of the bombardment, our school decided to leave London again. This time they put us in a dank and cheerless mansion in the north of England. Certainly it was safe. We could not imagine even the most determined SS commander wanting to invade that dreary corner of Cheshire in the middle of what turned out to be the worst winter weather for 20 years.

But how tedious it was. Instead of the cosy beds at Bexhill we were herded into bleak unheated dormitories. The teachers, whose authority over us would previously have expired mid-afternoon, now wielded power around the clock.

In spring we persuaded our parents to bring us back home and we joined another school that had stayed put in defiance of the war. This was a far more cheery place than our previous school. When sirens wailed we moved down to the basement and sang songs like "Old Macdonald" instead of conjugating Latin verbs.

Eventually the nightly Blitz tailed off as Hitler inexplicably switched his attention to the Soviet Union. Air raids continued on a much more sporadic scale although German fighters returning home would sometimes strafe suburban streets rather than take back unspent ammunition. On one such occasion a Messerschmidt 109 swooped over our home at Merchiston Road, Catford. Lying flat in the hallway I was astonished to see our elderly neighbour, one Mrs Clitter who normally hobbled along with the aid of a stick, sprinting like an Olympic ace along the pavement before hurling herself across her own garden hedge. The pilot soared away having failed to get Mrs Clitter.

∙∙∙∙∙∙∙∙∙∙

Kate Soar continues her memories of life in Oldham, Lancashire:

Houses were blacked out and my mother became worried about feeding us properly. We had to carry gas masks and I wore an identity bracelet but it was amazing how much of life was maintained.

On Christmas Day 1940 we spent the evening with my aunt and uncle who lived ten minutes walk away. The adults were determinedly jolly as planes droned overhead, anti-aircraft guns blazed, shrapnel tinkled as it hit the ground and there was a lot of dull, explosive noise.

My sister, aged seven, got at the sherry and performed a hilarious cabaret before falling asleep. When we left, the horizon from left to right was totally crimson, like an extended sunset, because Manchester was on fire. That was very sobering.

I remember one of the senior boys coming back to the school in uniform with an empty sleeve, or was it just an arm in a sling. Rumours flew that he had been wounded by the enemy.

When France fell, we sang "God Save the King" in assembly, with special emphasis on "Scatter his enemies, And make them fall." I remember thinking that the Channel was very narrow on the maps. At that point I'd hardly been out of Lancashire.

As part of the war effort I had picked peas in Ormskirk. We had camped in bell tents, organised by what I can now recognise as a noble group of women teachers. It was for girls only, though the school was co-ed.

....

Life, for Mary Norsworthy, continued in the quiet village of Riseley in Bedfordshire that she and her family had been evacuated to. Despite the continued progression of the war, she still found plenty of fun and mischief around her.

When the Germans started bombing the south with V2 rockets, hundreds of families left coastal towns. A family called Vance come and squeezed in with us. Mrs Vance and her five or six children, the two teachers and the four of us were all living in this tiny cottage.

Dad was always digging a big hole in the garden to empty the lavatory bucket. Our vegetable garden thrived! My brother Michael, whom I adored, had some great ideas and inventions. He made a parachute from a tablecloth and said I could go down in history by being the first to jump from the roof of the barn. I did, and was nearly history. Then he decided to give me driving lessons in our car, one of very few in the village. Michael said the first thing was to take the brake off. The car gently rolled down the drive and through the barn door.

We received various parcels from the United States containing chocolate powder, bundles of clothes and malted milk tablets. Twenty-five years later, my American husband told me that he was asked at school to bring clothes and canned goods to send bundles to Britain. I may have even worn a pair of his socks.

Michael told me that if I showed my bottom to the village boys, they would give me some of their malted milk tablets. I did but I never saw a malted milk tablet. What is more Michael told my parents what I had done, the sneak.

I remember the cottage with great affection. There were always lots of people there and it was lots of fun. When we were offered the chance to buy the cottage at the end of the war for £200 my parents reluctantly turned it down. How different our lives would have been had we stayed.

Thurleigh was the closest US air base to the village. There were a few camps around all guarded by US servicemen. We would often go to the barrier and ask the guard in Americanese: "Got any gum chum?"

My mother worked in the PX stores which meant she could occasionally sneak out with some ice cream or other goodies. I remember a time she came home with a tin of condensed milk. She opened it and gave Michael and me a spoon each and told us to eat it. I can still remember that taste.

Mother would talk about famous people who were based at Thurleigh - Clark Gable and Glenn Miller being two. I often heard conversations of Memphis Belle – the now famous aeroplane, although I don't think it flew from Thurleigh.

We saw mainly Flying Fortresses and would watch them fly out on a mission, dozens of them – an incredible sight. We would then wait for them to return and watch for our particular friends' planes. We knew the big numbers on their sides. Seeing these planes come in was a distressing sight. Many were so badly shot up it was amazing they could still fly. The engines would be faltering or on fire and frequently one could see great holes in the wings, tail or fuselage. Sometimes one would crash before it reached the base, I remember one crashing in a garden in the village. It remained there for what seemed a long time, days or weeks, and we all went to see it and take some of the Perspex glass. This we would make into rings for our fingers by using red-hot pokers to make the holes and designs.

One story I heard much later in life about Thurleigh concerned a visit by King George VI and Princess Elizabeth. The weeks prior to their visit had seen many outbreaks of VD on the base, and the base commander ordered that the barracks that had the most cases of the disease in a week would be made to fly a yellow flag with VD blazoned on it.

On escorting the King and Queen round the base the officers were horrified to see a yellow flag still flying. The Queen spotted this and asked what it was for. After a short silence, a young officer stepped forward and said 'Victory Drive, Mam.' I'll bet he ended up a general.

My father was a great organiser and, within a short space of time, he had put together a theatre group which would perform and win prizes in competitions around Bedfordshire. He also organised picture shows, lectures, dances and socials. The lovely thing about these evenings was that the whole village turned up to join in, and many of the GIs too. I was always first on stage when the conjuror asked for a member of the audience to come and help him.

One terrible night when Michael and I were at a social event run by my father, a beautiful iced cake was raffled by a villager. We had not seen a cake like this for many years and our mouths watered. The time came to draw the winning ticket and my father won it.

Michael and I were ecstatic jumping up and down with excitement. It was short-lived. I heard my father say ' Draw again, we don't want it'. It was then won by a GI, who tore the cake apart in front of our eyes. Talking to my brother about our memories we both remember that *incident so vividly, we never quite forgave our father for that. When telling my own children this story they found it hard to believe.*

....

A new generation had been born that never knew life in any other situation than the war. Margaret Juett was born in November 1938 in a small village near the coast in West Sussex, and cut her first tooth on the day war broke out. Her earliest memories were of a life in the midst of war:

As a small child, I could not remember a time before the war and so took for granted such things as identity cards, ration books, the blackout and air raid sirens. I remember trying to puzzle out how my parents and I had somehow got consecutive identity numbers - I thought that everyone had always had them.

As my dad was in a reserved occupation and nearly 40, he wasn't called up, but worked long hours and was in the Home Guard. So although I saw him only at weekends – he left and returned while I was asleep – I didn't have to cope with his enforced absence for months or years, as many of my contemporaries did.

We had been living on a road that had become part of Ford Naval Air Station. It became too dangerous to stay there so we moved out to stay with friends until we could rent a house in the next village for the duration of the war. We ended up there until 1953.

The air raids are usually the most vivid memory for children, and I am no exception. When the siren sounded my mother would send me to hide under either the sink or the solid oak kitchen table. The sink was an old-fashioned type: shallow yellow stone supported on brick pillars and so probably able to withstand bricks and rubble falling on it.

When I was about four years old my great aunt Adelaide came from Yorkshire to stay with us. She wasn't used to air raids. One afternoon she took me for a walk in my pushchair up to Tye Lane. We turned at the top of the hill to watch the planes darting and zooming in the sky. When we got home, my mother was in a flat panic. There had been an air raid warning and we had been watching a dog fight between British and German planes.

The most frightening occasion was when I was five or six. During the night, after I had gone to bed, I was awoken by my parents and hurried downstairs to hide behind a large armchair in the corner of the sitting room where the chimney stacks rose through the house – the best place for all three of us to hide. We could hear the sounds of planes and anti-aircraft fire and it was coming closer. The plane's engines cut out above us. I remember my mum and dad urgently whispering to each other about whether my father should risk going to fetch the wood panel to fix against the window to protect us from flying glass. I realised they were very afraid.

The German plane crashed in the field behind our house. When things had calmed down there came a knock at the door. A policeman had been sent to check we were alright and to tell us what had happened. I was terrified because, at the time, I was being bullied at school by a boy who had threatened to send the police to me if I didn't give him a sweet. I thought that his threat had come true when the policeman arrived!

The next day our village was pervaded by a smell of petrol. The army was everywhere. I was sent to spend the day with friends in the next village as it transpired that there had been two unexploded bombs on the plane when it crashed, and the pilot had landed in a tree. In the following week, all the local children invaded the area to pick up bits of twisted metal and shattered glass as souvenirs.

....

Some families considered evacuation of a different sort – not just leaving cities for the country, but leaving Britain completely for the duration of the war. David Owers was evacuated from his home town in Cuffley, Hertfordshire, to Canada with his mother and brother.

As evacuees, my mother, older brother and I, aged five, left Liverpool docks to cross the Atlantic in July 1940. It was to be two years before we would return from Canada.

My parents agreed that my father Leo would stay in England but my mother Thora should leave with us. Just six weeks earlier, at the end of May, the Dunkirk evacuation had taken place; the flotilla of little ships ferrying the majority of the expeditionary troops home. Paris was occupied mid-June, then a week later France conceded and the UK was alone. The reality of enemy forces massed directly across the Channel would have concentrated everyone's minds, especially that of a parent. But what a decision to confront!

The political advice was clear. Grandparents and fathers should stay; but children were to be moved well away from London and the southeast, and quickly. For evacuation abroad, passenger liners were commissioned and filled with mothers and children for the long voyage across the North Atlantic to carers organised by the Red Cross in

Canada or the USA. If faced with such a decision now, would my wife and I have chosen the most traumatic option involving division of the family for an unknown period of time? The decision had to be taken quickly, not least because of the logistics involved.

Our home in Cuffley, Hertfordshire, was hardly a priority target, merely the possible recipient of a bombing over-run. (There is a memorial in Cuffley at the site where Zeppelin SL11, one of a bomb-carrying flotilla of airships, crashed in flames in WW1.)

Churchill's resounding words "... fighting them on the beaches ... in the hills..." wonderfully stiffened the backbone and the heart; yet awareness of the realities of the late 1930s had filtered through by then, and only an uninformed minority would favour the odds of isolated Britain back then.

We travelled by train to Liverpool Docks to embark on the liner 'Duchess of Atholl'. The ship was packed and we were directed endlessly downwards into the depths of the hull, with seemingly nothing but bilgewater and keel below.

The dangerous voyage to the St. Lawrence River, Canada, was to last nearly two weeks. The 'Duchess' was totally unescorted but she made the journey safely, despite U-boat activity. Sadly it was a different story for other ships.

Having my mother and brother with me made things seem normal. But contrast this, however, with the unhappy lot of the sole unaccompanied child similarly venturing into the unknown. My memory of the trip is mostly restricted to that steep descent into the depths of the hull clutching a clumsy cork life jacket and also of an uncomfortable scrubbing in a salt water bath or two.

The Family Owers were allocated to Port Credit west of Toronto – to be billeted eventually in the gatehouse of an extensive estate owned by the Adamson family on the shores of Lake Ontario.

The lakeside setting provided a captivating playground. In summer we would swim in the lake and in winter, we would explore the first few hundred feet of frozen lake wrapped in our fur-lined gear.

Marshland by the oil depot would be flooded to form an ice rink where, with ice hockey sticks, we raced around after the puck and the opposing team.

I learned many things the hard way: on the estate lawn I discovered the sting incurred from treading on a bee; in the woods, that rattlesnakes were to be avoided and that tender unclothed skin in contact with poison ivy produced remarkably long lasting irritation.

Mum coped as a single mother has to, and no doubt she appreciated the North American standard of living, which contrasted sharply with that left behind. In many respects it was an idyllic interlude in childhood. I have many lasting impressions of my time there such as the journeying due north for holidays in vast fir-wooded territory near Algonquin Park and staying in a real log cabin.

We made regular trips, across the placid Lake Kashagawigamog by outboard motor-driven dinghy, for the nearest provisions and for mail collection.

By 1942 Mum and Dad had a plan for our return to the UK. But propaganda had suppressed the realities of the war at sea. The risks associated with a return crossing of the North Atlantic would not have been fully appreciated by my parents when they decided to do it. In July 1942 an Atlantic crossing by convoy took around three weeks.

With the introduction earlier that year of a fourth ring on the Enigma encoders, serving the U-boat hunter packs, Bletchley code breaking was again in a 'blind' state. Our ragged flotilla, moving at the speed of the slowest, zigzagged repeatedly but still lost a third of its merchant ships. However, we were safely positioned on the Commodore's destroyer at the apex of the convoy. There was one other civilian family on board, plus one hundred Royal Air Force newly trained bomber crew, mostly around twenty years old.

In the mornings, they gave us lessons in Morse code. Then they would amuse us by making elaborate balsa wood models of guns, tanks and aircraft.

They told mum to look after herself if anything should happen and that they would see to the kids. They were good travel companions and she kept in touch with them the following year. Sadly, it emerged that only six of the 100 survived in the bomber command raids for more than a year.

We docked in Belfast and were ferried happily to Liverpool, the three of us complete with large brass bound trunks, from where we took a train to meet Dad in London. Thora, formerly a reticent, no doubt dutiful but self-effacing wife, had adopted the can-do mannerisms of her host country over two years. When the train arrived at Euston she commandeered a baggage transporter, saw the trunks and her boys aboard and rode shotgun astride a trunk, whooping it up as we approached Dad at the gate. It must have taken him weeks to adjust to his newly independent-minded wife.

We too had to readjust – we were back to rationing with food and clothing coupons, to blackouts, gas masks, and air-raid sirens for 'doodle bugs' – but we were back!

David Owers as a young boy in 1939

The effects of the war in Europe were felt across the globe, even in countries not directly involved. Peter Carolin, a ten-year-old British boy living in Brazil, may have experienced the war second-hand, but it was very real to his family. He recalls the atmosphere there after Britain declared war on Germany.

My uncle's RAF Bristol Blenheim bomber (L8776) was shot down over the Netherlands on the day that country was invaded, 10 May 1940. Our German nanny was dismissed shortly after the news of his capture reached my mother. It was, for me, the start to a rather unreal war.

We lived in Rio de Janeiro. My Anglo-Irish father worked for a British firm whose operations were based in Brazil. My (mainly) Scots mother's family had lived and worked in the Argentine, Uruguay and Brazil for many years – indeed, my sister and I were the fifth generation to be born in South America.

In May 1940, when I was three and my sister was two, our nanny Thea Guenzburger or Mitti Bickles as we called her, was forced to leave our household. We were devoted to her and she to us so there was much distress at her enforced departure. Ironically, she was Jewish - and a photographer by training - who had left Germany because of the Nazis. We neither saw her again nor knew what happened to her – something that worries me to this day.

There was a large British community in Brazil and an even larger German one. The country was, in effect, a dictatorship presided over by Getulio Vargas – a man with more than a little admiration for the Fascist states of Europe. Brazilians, like any other nation, prefer to be on the winning side and this had an unfortunate consequence: during the early years of the war, some Brazilians would spit as we passed in the street with my mother because we were British.

Later on, when the Allies were clearly winning (and the Germans had made the big mistake of sinking some Brazilian ships), Brazil entered the war on the Allied side and sent an expeditionary force to fight in Italy. Unfortunately, because of our blond hair some Brazilians assumed we must be German – so the spitting continued.

At one stage, the hostility towards the British threatened to become so serious that the Embassy advised the British community to lay in stocks of essentials and be prepared to stay in their homes until a British cruiser came to take them off. My mother, convinced that our water would be cut off, laid in vast stocks of mineral water. Three years later, after the tide of war had turned and we were about to move from the house in which we lived on Ipanema beach, we still had vast stocks of mineral water: my sister and I remember being made to use it while cleaning our teeth. My grandmother's big buy was toilet paper. Her flat was filled with the stuff and there was still some there when they retired to England five years after the war.

The possibility of a British cruiser picking us up from Copacabana beach must have seemed somewhat remote to adults acutely aware of the Royal Navy's over-stretched resources. The one regular link back to Britain (or 'Home' as it used to be called in these expatriate communities) had been the elegant passenger liners of the Royal Mail and Blue Star lines and, as the war went on and I grew older, I would hear how so many of these had been lost.

Cruisers and armed merchant cruisers did, of course, call in to Rio for rapid re-provisioning, refuelling and recreation. The first of these was HMS Ajax on its way back to Britain after the battle of the River Plate in December 1939. I have no memory of that but I do of others (such as the Birmingham and the Despatch), of the wonderful children's parties that, astonishingly, they laid on for us – and of the officers who came to spend a day or two at home. There was always a big group of us down at the port to see them off with their smart khaki-uniformed, white pith-helmeted Royal Marine contingents lined up on the quarterdeck.

Every so often, we would go down to the port to see off a ship filled with 'volunteers' – young Britons, men and women, in their late teens and early twenties going to Britain to enlist. My twenty-year-old aunt was among them. My grandfather, then 51, had joined the Home Guard when called to Britain in 1941. Thus, as a child remote from the home front, I sensed a very strong feeling of commitment to Britain. One of the most dramatic manifestations of this was the sight of literally hundreds of Empire troops – South Africans, Australians and New Zealanders – crowding the decks of the vast Queen Mary, anchored for a brief stay in the bay at Rio.

As the very young Chairman of the British Community Council, my father raised substantial sums of money to pay for fighters for the RAF. As a reward, he was allowed to suggest names and I recall a photograph of a Spitfire with the curious name, to non-Portuguese speakers, of Filha da Puta. Translated, this means 'Son of a Bitch' – quite appropriate for a fighter.

Later on, the Council bought a little yellow Piper Cub for the Brazilian Air Force. Tactfully, it was named after a local politician.

****

CHAPTER FIVE
WAR-TIME RECOLLECTIONS OF GERMAN CHILDREN

The experiences of children living in Germany under the Nazis in the years leading up to and during the war were far from normal. Once the Americans joined the war, the Germans too experienced bombing similar to that which had destroyed communities in Britain and other parts of Europe.

Konrad Gittinger describes his experience as a young boy living in Nazi Germany:

I was born in 1938 in a small town in the Black Forest in Southern Germany. I was the youngest child in a family consisting of two sisters and three brothers. The same year my mother was awarded a medal for mothers – the Mutterkreuz – which I presume she was given for producing six children.

My faint recollection of the war goes back to early 1944. At that time my father, who was a captain of the "Großdeutsches Heee" (German army), went missing in action in Romania. My mother was on compulsory state service with a company called "Hautana" sewing uniforms for the

German army. She also helped out in a nearby military hospital on a voluntary basis. My 17-year-old sister worked in the Polish territory, then under German rule, as a household aid in a so-called "kinderreiche Familie" (a family with a great number of children). My 16- year-old brother was a "Flakhelfer" (a member of the Luftwaffe) assistant in an army battery in Bavaria. He was already registered as a future volunteer in the German airforce, so he might avoid a possible service in the Waffen-SS.

My 14-year-old sister and my nine-year-old brother were at home, both still too young for any compulsory state service. However my sister was a member of the Bund Deutscher Mädel a Hitler youth organisation for girls aged up to 18 and my brother a member of the "Deutsches Jungvolk" for eight to 14-year-old boys.

I was still too young to join the Deutsches Jungvolk, but I very much envied my nine-year-old brother as he had a nice uniform with a brown shirt and black trousers, a belt with a marked belt buckle, a water bottle and a little spade for field activities.

Until the end of the war, we had always enough to eat – even white bread, which was a luxury in those days.

I still remember the year 1944, when big fleets of allied bombers flew over our town night and day, generally heading in a southern direction, most likely heading for Offenburg and Freiburg. There were quite a lot of air-raid alarms towards the end of the war. I can still remember one allied air raid when some bombs were dropped near our house but luckily there was little damage. However, a town called Pforzheim, which was some 50 km to the north of us, seemed to be bombed nightly. I vividly remember one particular night when we could clearly see an inferno there with a reddish-tinged sky. We were always told not to pick up anything from the street after an air raid and warned that the allied air forces would drop fountain-pens and toys containing explosives.

In autumn 1944 I started school. My first schoolbook ("Fibel") had nice pictures of members of the Nazi party and the Deutsches Jungvolk marching and camping. I still recall one specific reading exercise starting with "Hi..Hi..Hi..Hitler".

From time to time, all school members had to go to the fields near our town to collect beetles that were harming the potato crops. We were told that the beetles had been dropped by the allied air force.

In those days one could also find quite a lot of allied leaflets on the fields asking German soldiers to surrender. However we were strictly forbidden to pick them up by the Nazi party. Strips of tinfoil (called chaffs) came showering down from the skies dropped by the allied air forces. These were to interfere with the German radar.

In late 1944, the husband of our household aid, who was a railway official, arrested an allied pilot with plain clothes on a train heading to our town. He was subsequently awarded the "Kriegsverdienstkreuz 2 Klasse ohne Schwerter" medal (a minor medal for non-combattants) which he proudly wore. I was very impressed.

By early 1945 we still had learned nothing about the whereabouts of my father. The rest of the family was now all back at home. At this time, I was still deeply convinced that Germany would win the war, perhaps because of the Nazi propaganda machine's claims that numerous V2 rockets had caused very big damages in London.

My 16-year-old brother, having been temporarily released from the army battery, wanted to show my brother and I how explosives worked and so he put them in the well in front of our house and set them off. The bang was remarkable. So far nothing worth mentioning had happened in our town, so the ensuing reaction was one of panic. The fire brigade and local party officials rushed to the scene of the explosion where my mother then had to explain that this was only a piece of folly and not the action of an allied spy.

To protect him from the local Nazi party or the SS, my mother made an agreement with the local leader that my brother should immediately join the "Volkssturm" (a militia of armed local people set up to help with defending local areas). While on duty, he was taken prisoner by the French army and was temporarily kept in his old school as a French prisoner of war before being used as a farm labourer in France. He didn't return for three years until 1948.

The day before the end of the war, the Nazi party distributed posters and leaflets telling everyone to leave the town immediately.

However they forgot to tell us which direction to go in. As far as I can remember, this advice was ignored by everybody, since the US army had also advanced some 20km to the East of the town (stopping a further advance by the French army towards Stuttgart). To protect our valuables, my mother dug out holes in a rather foul smelling rubbish dump in our garden. All the family silver, other valuables and bottles of French brandy went into these holes.

The following night the French army conquered our town with Sherman tanks and attached colonial troops. They advanced from the West via the Schloßberg – a hill with the ruins of a castle on top overlooking the town. All the tank barriers set up by the Volkssturm on the main roads leading to the town had been erected in vain. As far as I know there had been no resistance whatsoever from the population, since the German army had already disintegrated (not to mention Göring's Luftwaffe).

The French soldiers, who consisted mostly of Moroccans led by French officers, shouted "Itler kaputt, Krieg aus" (which literally meant "Hitler broken, war over").

When the French soldiers arrived in our town, we were hiding in the cellar of our house. My mother and my two sisters had all darkened their faces and hands with soot and earth. When we left our cellar during the night, we discovered that our house had been partly looted, most notably the Leica camera which belonged to my father was missing. However the valuable contents buried in the rubbish dump in our garden had not been found. The next morning, the place in front of our house was crowded with Moroccan soldiers who were roasting mutton over open fires. The following day the French army occupied part of our house using it as an office which made the house safer. The French soldiers were very kind to me and later on I had extensive conversations with them, although I did not have much knowledge of the French language.

The day after the French occupied our house, a neighbour (who was a noodle maker) shouted "Du Nazi Sau" (you Nazi swine) at my mother. A day later he apologised and presented us with 2kg of noodles, which were very costly in those days.

Evidently there wasn't just looting going on the night the French army arrived – nine months later some very Moroccan-looking, new-born babies arrived.

Being former members of the "NS Frauenschaft" (the female organisation of the NSDAP) my mother and other local women were chosen to clear the rubbish dump of the town under the watch of a communist. But they were soon released from their duties.

Following the war, food became scarce. Anything from shops or public buildings that was not guarded was looted. Throughout the following winter we lived mostly on turnips and some of the family silver and other valuables had to be exchanged for food. Care parcels and food supplies from the United States came much later.

The German army had left an anti aircraft gun and lots of ammunition, tin helmets and other military equipment in front of our house. We had great fun playing with these war leftovers. We opened the rifle and tank ammunition and made big fires with the contents. I had hidden some machine gun ammunition under my bed, but was made to put it into the nearby river when my mother discovered it.

Other children were less fortunate. A five-year-old boy from our neighbourhood lost his fingers after playing with an anti-aircraft gun. Also a six-year-old boy lost his life playing with ammunition and another boy lost his right leg. By the end of 1945 we got a letter from the Red Cross in Russia informing us that my father was still alive. But it wasn't until 1954 that he returned from Russian captivity in Stalingrad where he had been working since 1945 as an enforced labourer.

Konrad Gittinger, left, with his brother and father, before his father was captured by the Russians and made to work in one of the labour camps.

· · · · · · · · ·

Sisters Hannelore Williams and Roswitha Frey remember completely different aspects of the war as they were ten years apart in age. Hannelore became a member of the Hitler Youth before the war broke out. As she recalled:

We lived in a village in Westfalen in Germany when Hitler became Chancellor in 1933. I was then 11 years old. My father worked at the Catholic Elementary School. I joined the "Jung Madels" around that time. This was a Hitler Youth organisation for young girls.

I enjoyed wearing the uniform and taking part in the sports and singing, which we had at our regular meetings. Music (singing) and athletics were my favourite subjects in high school, so I enjoyed these activities with the Jung Madels.

During my adolescent years I had no negative feelings against National Socialism and saw no reason to question or doubt anything I heard or read. When my one Jewish classmate disappeared from class around 1935, neither I, nor anyone in the class, questioned why she was no longer there.

That same year my father took me to Kassel, where he was born, to visit his parents and sister. His sister and husband were anti-Nazis and we visited Jewish friends with them. We listened to a speech Hitler made and they commented - naturally - against it. I was devastated. My father consoled me later by promising that I did not have to visit his hometown again.

Hannah's younger sister Roswitha Frey has vivid memories of being bombed: *When the war broke out, I was living with my father as my parents had separated early in 1941.*

I will never forget watching that American bomber crash in 1942. I was nine years old living in the Ruhr area in a village called Opherdicke. It was built on a hill that overlooked the industrial region of the Ruhrgebiet. With its steel production plants and coal mines the area was a prime target for the Allies. A number of anti-aircraft units were stationed around the village and they drew frequent attacks from the fighter planes that accompanied the slower-flying bombers.

This was a daytime raid of B-53 bombers. When the plane crashed everyone who witnessed it, including myself, rushed to the bomber. In the shattered cockpit we found the pilot was still alive. Men from a nearby garrison extricated the pilot and carried him on a stretcher to a nearby inn.

The officer in charge knew I spoke English (I was the daughter of the Principle of the local school) and so he asked me to translate their questions and the prisoner's answers. I felt intense compassion for the unfortunate man, although death and bloody injuries were commonplace then.

As the war progressed and night-time bombing became continuous, I was evacuated with other girls of varying ages to Freudenstadt, in the Black Forest. The Kindertransport made us feel like we were on a camping trip as we were in a rural setting with fresh air and better food than we were used to. Away from the bombing, we enjoyed uninterrupted sleep. We slept in dormitories and were divided into groups of 10 with a teacher or matron in charge. Classes were often held out of doors as there was not enough classroom space. For most of us, homesickness was the major problem. With so many girls together, a clique system developed and the older girls kept us in line and took it upon themselves to tell us the facts of life. I cannot recall exactly how long we stayed there but in 1945, with approaching puberty, the courts decided I should return to my mother. She had by then returned to her home town, Baiersbronn, in the Black Forest, so was close to where the Kindertransport had brought us.

During the last weeks of the war, my mother and I were caught between the battle lines. It was during the Easter vacation and mother was taking me from Westfalia to Hessia where she was teaching. I had a bad strep throat and high fever so it was impossible to travel. We were staying with friends who had a grocery store when British units with artillery and tanks moved through the Rhineland.

The German local defenders had drafted anyone between 16 and 70 as militia and were determined not to surrender. We faced 36 hours of artillery barrage and tank fire. During this continuous bombardment the cellar of the house in which we were hiding nearly became our grave since the house took several hits.

When we tried to scramble through the dust and rubble we found that the pharmacy across the street had also been hit and chemicals were exploding and burning, making our escape even more harrowing. We made a mad dash in groups of two between explosions to the town hall as it had extensive air raid shelter space. We were found by British Forces who had come in search of deserters and anyone with a rifle.

At that time, Germany was occupied by the Allies and divided into four zones - American, British, French and Russian. My mother's home was in the American zone but we were currently in the British zone. There was no public transport available so we were forced to walk for several hundred kilometres to get home which took several weeks. Along the way we had to identify ourselves whenever we entered another town or village and explain why we were on the road. There were checkpoints on all routes. You needed a pass to go from one place to anywhere outside your town or village, and curfews were strictly enforced. On one road a group of former Polish prisoners were armed with guns in order to rob anyone coming by. One of them, seeing a woman and child thought we were an easy target and barred our way with his gun. Believing him to be American or British I addressed him in English, which surprised him. He consulted the rest of his group and then asked in German if we had anything of value. I replied in English that we were refugees and had nothing they could use. It was not unusual for refugees of different nationalities to be on the move, which probably made them let us go, but my heart was in my throat and I looked back to make sure they didn't change their minds about letting us pass unharmed.

Only the kindness of strangers and the fact that we bartered our few possessions for food along the way made it possible to reach home. What I as a child noticed was that the Americans often gave us part of their C-rations, such as chocolate, raisins and cookies. The reason I eventually moved to America, where I still live, was because of my impression that Americans, even during wartime, were capable of being humane and willing to help, which was not the case with others.

By the time we reached home we were in bad shape. I had worn through two pairs of shoes, the last of which I had to enlarge by cutting out the front to accommodate my swollen, blistered feet.

****

CHAPTER SIX
THE PACIFIC WAR BEGINS: EVACUATION FROM HONG KONG

The war in Europe provided Japan with an opportunity to take over Asian territories occupied by European countries without resistance. Japan had a huge population but very little natural resources and had for a long time cast an envious eye on Asian territories occupied by the Americans and Europeans.

For years Japan had been taking advantage of any weaknesses in other countries to expand its empire. They had occupied and ruled Korea and Formosa (now Taiwan) since 1895 - which now provided much of Japan's rice and other agricultural needs.

In 1932, virtually unopposed by the Chinese, whose Nationalist and Communist armies were busy fighting each other, the Japanese captured and occupied the whole of Manchuria. Japan particularly coveted Shanghai, China's largest city and the centre for industry. They invaded Shanghai in 1932 but were forced to withdraw by the League of Nations.

Shanghai was originally created in 1842 by the Treaty of Nanking, which ended the Opium War and prepared the way for the opening up of China.

The treaty granted foreigners the right to settle there and in certain ports. Shanghai quickly became the most important port and was the world's gateway to China.

In 1933 the American ambassador in Tokyo reported to Washington that Japanese children's schoolbooks were being published showing the Phillippines, Malaya, Singapore, the Dutch East Indies, French Indochina and Siam (now Thailand) to be under the Rising Sun Flag - that they were Japanese possessions.

Fighting broke out between the Japanese and Chinese in 1937 and the Japanese invaded and captured Peking (now Beijing). They also bombarded Shanghai. Fighting the Chinese in this vast country with long-drawn battle lines, was exhausting the Imperial Army. Which was why they began to turn their eyes to the easier and more alluring prizes that lay to the southeast.

The USA and Britain, in an attempt to halt Japan's expansionistic plans, had imposed sanctions on certain raw materials being exported to Japan. But with Britain fighting for survival in Europe, it became clear that it could not defend their colonies. Singapore was considered impregnable, but the Governor of Hong Kong had been told that Hong Kong could not expect any help from Britain in defending the territory.

In 1940 the Governor of Hong Kong decided that as the colony could not be defended, they should not have any *bouches inutile* - useless mouths - and the safest and wisest course would be to evacuate women and children while it was still possible. So more than a year before the inevitable hostilities broke out, women and children were evacuated to safer areas - usually to Australia.

As a child of five, author of this book Helen Massey (Née Bendall) was among the first to leave Hong Kong with her brothers and mother. Their father was an accountant working for the colonial office, and probably had no choice about when to leave.

Helen Massey recalls her departure from Hong Kong:

The day was grey and my parents were quiet. We were sitting on the deck of a ship in Hong Kong harbour. Our ahma (child minder), Ah Ho, was also there, and she tried to cheer us up with strips of dessicated coconut she produced from a paper bag.

I was five and had three brothers, Roy aged eight, Gordon three, and baby John was just a few months old. We sat silently. Neither of my parents explained why we were there. Then my father and Ah Ho got up to leave and there were quick hugs and kisses.

I didn't know it then but it would be over five years before I would see my father again – as he was to become a Japanese prisoner of war – and nine years before I would return to Hong Kong.

After my father left the ship, my mother hurried us into the lounge staking claim to a sofa and several armchairs. We did not have a cabin or bed between the five of us. The ship, the Empress of Asia, *set sail and all I can remember of the journey was sleeping on the floor of the lounge. Some days later we steamed into Manila in the Phillippines.*

On arrival, Red Cross workers took us to a hotel. We were given a small, very dark room with one single bed in it. There was also an armchair. My mother put three of us in the bed, like sardines, head to tail. Baby John had his pram and mother sat up all night in the chair. Throughout the night we heard doors banging and noisy footsteps along the corridor. Next day my mother - who never made waves - was furious. Years later I overheard her telling someone that we had been placed in a brothel.

From there we were taken in one of a fleet of canvas-topped lorries to Fort McKinley, a US army camp. It was raining and we all felt miserable. When we arrived we were taken to a long Nissen hut with a row of camp beds along each side. This was to be our home for the next few months. There was little to do - no books or anything to play with.

At meal times we queued up at a counter where dollops of food were plonked on our tin plates. I could only just see over the counter top, but when I saw cabbage being dished up, I kept my plate out of the way. What joy that gave me!

I have no idea exactly how long we stayed there but it always seemed to be raining. Our next move was to board a Dutch ship called the Christian Huygens. We set sail for Sydney, Australia, and this time we were allocated a cabin.

I shall never forget entering Sydney Harbour early one morning. I was so excited that I got up early and stood on deck as we sailed slowly under the majestic Sydney Harbour Bridge. I remember looking up, terrified that the ship's masts were too high and would hit the underside of the bridge. But they cleared it and we gently turned left to moor at the docks.

I have often thought how difficult it must have been for my mother with a baby, toddler and a five and eight year old. What did she do about nappies, baby food, laundry? Sadly I never got to ask those questions.

Arriving at Sydney she had no idea what would happen to us next. But the Red Cross once more took over and we were taken to 23 Queen Street, in the suburb of Mosman, where we shared one room in a small boarding house run by a Miss Hamilton and her brother, George.

There was only one other resident, an elderly lady called Miss Constable. Later I learned she was the granddaughter of the famous artist.

In summer we often went to the local beach, Balmoral. It had a small area protected by netting to keep away sharks so mother felt happier with us there. Occasionally she became more adventurous and took us to Manly and Bondi beaches.

We loved going on trams. Like the ones in San Francisco, they were open at the sides and the conductor would swing along the outside platform to collect the fares. We particularly liked crossing Sydney Harbour Bridge on a tram. And we loved Taronga Park Zoo, where we could ride on an elephant and walk along paths looking up at koala bears high in the branches of gum trees.

The Japanese war still had not started so we had regular letters from my father and there was a relaxed and contented atmosphere.

....

Above: Helen Massey (Née Bendall) with brothers (clockwise from left: Roy, Gordon and John Bendall) as refugees in Australia.
Right: Their father, James Bendall, remained in Hong Kong and became a member of Hong Kong's police reserves before he was captured by the Japanese and held as a prisoner of war.

Joan Franklin was also evacuated from Hong Kong around the same time: *Shortly after my fifth birthday, I realised that preparations were being made for me to leave Hong Kong, together with my mother, older brother and sister. My father, Freddy Franklin, who worked for the Hong Kong newspapers, The Daily Telegraph and the South China Morning Post, was remaining behind. Rather than join the Royal Hong Kong Volunteer Regiment, he joined The Royal Engineers, and in due course was captured by the Japanese.*

He was wounded and spent some time in the Bowen Road Military Hospital prior to being interned by the Japanese in Shamshuipo and Argyle Street military camps. He had already served in World War I, in France, and was over 50 years of age at the beginning of World War II.

We left Hong Kong on a passenger liner, called the Neptuna, in August 1940 at night time. There were blackout curtains over the portholes and instead of the customary bright lights on board, the light bulbs were blue, which gave a strange and eerie incandescent light.

Our first port of call was Saigon. During the day mother took me ashore and we rode in a small horse-driven carriage. Suddenly mother called out in French to the driver to stop, as she had seen a horseshoe on the road. To the driver's amazement she got him to pick it up for her as she considered it an omen of good luck. In the evening I remained on board ship, watching mother from the railing, as she and other passengers walked up and down the wharf, their cigarette ends glowing in the dark.

We disembarked at Sydney, Australia, not knowing that we were to be there for the next five and a half years.

··········

Michael Fingalson left Hong Kong with his mother and sister in September 1940 when his father was on business in Shanghai. He was three years old and his sister Pam was 11. He recalls:

My mother packed three suitcases - one with clothes, one with food and one with valuables that she could sell. Everything else we owned in Hong Kong we lost - the house, the car, furniture and personal mementoes that could never be replaced.

We were sent to the Phillippines and were there for some weeks before sailing to Sydney, Australia. The Red Cross took care of us there but as refugees we were moved about quite a bit in the area. I cannot remember much but have vague memories of living in one room in a house where chickens were kept in the back garden. I also remember going to Bondi beach and getting the ferry to Manly beach.

My father joined us in 1942 and he got a job as a naval architect to a shipyard in Brisbane where we stayed for the remainder of the war. My sister and I went to a school there run by a couple of elderly ladies.

At the end of the war, my father returned to Hong Kong on his own and lived in the Peninsula Hotel. We followed in 1946 by which time I was nine years old. We lived in the hotel for almost two years until my father was able to get a flat in St George's Mansions, Argyle Street when finally, normality returned to our lives.

****

CHAPTER SEVEN
CONQUERING COLONIAL TERRITORIES AND CAPTURING PRISONERS OF WAR

Japan attacked suddenly, ferociously and successfully. Early on Sunday morning, 7 December 1941, aircraft flew over Pearl Harbor, Hawaii, and attacked the American fleet anchored there. Most of the ships were torpedoed and sunk and US aircraft were destroyed while they were still on the ground.

Shanghai was also attacked on the same day - three hours before Pearl Harbor. Hong Kong, Singapore, Malaya and the Phillippines were all attacked the following day.

Despite having cracked Japanese codes, the Americans were still taken completely by surprise by the suddenness of the invasion. President Roosevelt announced that it was a day that would live on in infamy. The commander of the Japanese fleet, Admiral Yamamoto, remarked: 'I fear we have woken a sleeping giant.'

Although many American troops were helping to fight the war in Europe, there was still significant numbers of American forces fighting in the Pacific. In May 1942, the Americans gave the Japanese fleet their first setback in the battle of the Coral Sea.

Then, a month later and only six months after Pearl Harbor, the Japanese advance across the Pacific was decisively halted in the battle of Midway – the fiercest sea battle of all. But it wasn't enough.

Within a year the Japanese controlled most of the Pacific region and, as the months turned into years, life for those who were captured became increasingly desperate.

Hong Kong and Macau

Paul Wong, then a boy just three years old, was not evacuated from Hong Kong before the war but witnessed the invasion. The 8th December 1941 – the day after the attack on Pearl Harbor – was burned into his memory:

Japanese bombers flew over the island, bombarding the dockyards and the houses below. A large bomb hit a house very close to ours and the explosion forced up our floor, splitting it down the middle before it settled down again. We were lucky not to be hit.

I was only three years old and we were living in a large apartment within a house in Causeway Bay, which belonged to my father's family. Just before the invasion my mother had left to return to China to her family. My three brothers and I were left in the care of my sister who, though only 14 years old, did her best to care for all of us while our father worked. The bombing went on for two weeks before the Japanese marched in from Canton, which was on the border of Hong Kong. When my two older brothers were allowed out of the house, they came back with stories of dead people lying all over the roads and the harbour filled with floating bodies.

With just a token military force and civilians called up as reserves, Hong Kong only held out until Christmas Day before surrendering. Paul continues:

Once the Japanese had taken over, they rounded up all the young Chinese men and put them in concentration camps. British soldiers and civilians were put into Stanley jail and concentration camps in various parts of the island and mainland.

My father, who had been educated at a Catholic school, spoke excellent English and worked as a foreman at a nearby Government warehouse, was kept on in his job by the Japanese because he was useful.

Food was in very short supply but because of my father's work, he was able to smuggle out food and goods that had not been documented. We were lucky that we were never hungry and had enough essential clothing to wear. Others suffered more and most lost family members.

Throughout the war I was never allowed out of the house. From my memories, the apartment was big enough to run around in and had a balcony. I used to lean my head out to look at the sky and the road below. But I don't remember seeing grass, or flowers, or the sea. I wasn't able to run about and kick a ball, or mix with people.

••••••••••

Also in Hong Kong when the Japanese invaded was John Monteiro whose family was Portugeuse. Japan had not declared war on Portugal so they were allowed to go to Portugal's island colony of Macau, not far down the coast from Hong Kong, where they were put in a refugee camp.

We fled Hong Kong in a real hurry. The Japanese would not allow us to leave with anything, so my parents hid some money in my baby shoes, and we sailed off with my older brother and sister to Macau with a boat load of other refugees. The Macau Government still have records of our arrival, and they logged down every single item we brought with us. I had the most possessions – two pairs of shoes, and four sets of clothes. We were so thankful just to get out.

I remember well my days at the refugee camp. It was, in a strange way, quite fun. We were free to go anywhere we wanted. My father worked for the Portuguese Red Cross to try and get us some money. We went to school there. We were free, we had our pride and self esteem.

We may have had very little to eat, but did not starve at all as we had lots of rice and veggies. I never saw butter and other items we take for granted today, and we had very little sugar until after the war. It's funny, thinking back, how happy and grateful we were with so little. Today, we have so much, and it seems harder to be satisfied.

Once we received a food package from the American people, which contained chocolates amongst other things. It was such a great taste sensation. There was one pack of chewing gum, and my family decided that I should be the one to have it. I must have chewed on that same piece of gum for six months. I kept it in a little tin box by my bedside when I was not showing off to other kids that I had an American chewing gum in my mouth.

· · · · · · · · ·

Singapore

John Ritchie was a four-year-old boy in early 1942, living in Singapore with his mother and father, who was a naval officer. He recounts:

Life in Singapore was very quiet and we felt safe. Although we knew families had been evacuated from Hong Kong, everyone had been assured that Singapore was well defended. We had the new battleship the Prince of Wales *based there as well as an aircraft carrier. And all the biggest guns were pointing out to sea ready to destroy an invading navy.*

The threat of the Japanese did not seem to apply to Singapore, so our parents were happy to stay on. After all, with England at war, where would we go?

Suddenly one day Japanese aircraft appeared out of nowhere. Bombs were dropping all around us. There were no shelters to run to so my mother rushed me into one of the big storm drains that were built to carry off the torrential rain you could get in Singapore. Parts were covered over by roads so it offered some protection.

After a couple of air raids we heard that there was a ship in the harbour about to set sail. My father managed to get my mother and I on board just before it left. By now aircraft were attacking all ships they could find, and our captain set a course dodging in between the archepelago of islands that abound in the South China Sea.

At first there were many boats around us but some were sunk and others chose a different direction. Eventually we were clear of the islands in open sea heading for Australia.

I remember another passenger ship was sailing with us. But one day it was torpedoed. We watched in horror but the captain couldn't stop to help. He would have made our ship an easy target for the submarines and would have put it and all the passengers at risk. So he had to steam on.

He sailed so far south we were almost into the Antartic before heading east along the south coast of Australia. Finally we arrived in Sydney - to safety.

....

The Phillippines

In the Phillippines, shocked commanders heard of the strike on Pearl Harbour and realised that they would be next. The air commander at Clark air base, knowing Japanese bombers would have to fly from Formosa, tried to get permission to bomb the airfields there. He was denied access to General MacArthur for some hours and then was refused permission immediately. It was then 10am. By 11am he was told to load up the bombers, but before a single one could get off the ground the Japanese bombers had arrived. Only four fighters managed to get into the air but were destroyed by Zero fighters escorting the bombers. The one chance to strike back was lost. By the end of the month the Japanese occupied Manila, the capital of the Phillippines.

Diana Webb was trapped on a ship in Manila Harbour with members of her family when the bombing began in the Phillippines. They were making a stop off whilst on a cruise from Shanghai. She explained:

No one could ever have predicted that when my family and I went on a cruise on one of grandfather's ships that it would turn into a six-year nightmare that pitchforked our wealthy family from riches to rags.

The year was 1941 and I was two years old. My grandfather was Eric Moller – a shipping magnate who owned a fleet of 39 cargo ships that plied all over the Far East. The Moller Line at that time was the largest privately-owned fleet of steamships in the world, all registered in London. My grandfather named all his ships after girls in the family. There was a Nancy Moller, a Hannah Moller and an Erica Moller. The family lived in Shanghai and had been there for 98 years – since 1843 – but Moller Shipping had offices all over the Far East.

When the Japanese declared war on Britain and the United States, my grandmother, my mother and I, my aunt Nancy and her husband Gary, plus their two children, were actually on board one of grandfather's ships for a trip to visit exotic ports around the China Seas. We were anchored in Manila, where we were off-loading our cargo, when the Japanese suddenly attacked. Our ship was trapped – whether it was damaged by a bomb or unable to sail because it was blocked in, I was too young to know.

When the bombing ended and the Americans retreated, the Japanese marched into Manila and commandeered our ship. My grandmother, mother and I were taken to a prisoner of war camp. Gary, my aunt Nancy's husband, was French which meant their family was not interned as Japan was not at war with France. Their oldest girl, Izzy, was my age, two, and the youngest just a baby. They found a small house in Manila and a Filipino girl called Nemesia helped them in return for food and shelter.

At that time there were two camps - Santa Tomaz, the civilian camp, and Bilibid, the military camp, which was nearer the docks. As Santa Tomaz was over-crowded, Granny, my mother and I were put into the military camp – Bilibid. After about six months, Granny, who was nearing 70, was allowed out to live with her daughter, who the Japanese considered French. But my mother and I had to stay.

While we were in the camp my aunt and uncle found the Japanese in Manila were becoming increasingly hostile to Europeans. They became frightened for their lives and decided to leave.

With Granny, a baby and toddler they were unable to take much with them. Carrying a few belongings they trekked up into the mountains where they found a cave in Baguio, about 15 miles inland.

It was hardly the surroundings my aunt had been brought up with, as her family at that time was immensely wealthy, but she and my uncle were practical people. The cave appeared to be dry and provided shelter from the torrential rain of the Phillippines, yet would be cool in the hot, humid months. They had only what they were able to carry and what they found. There was a convent nearby, which the nuns ran as a hospital, and the nuns also gave them a few things. Nemesia went with them, but eventually returned to Manila.

When I was about three I got dysentery very badly and the camp doctor said I was certain to die. My mother asked if I could go to my grandmother, and at least die with my family. At first they refused and said no one was to be allowed out of the camp - even a three-year-old dying of dysentery.

Before the war my grandfather had owned a house in Japan, at Hamasaki, near Nagasaki, and when my mother was young, she and her brothers and sisters used to spend holidays there. My mother spoke some Japanese and persuaded the camp commandant to allow my grandmother to fetch me. Eventually he agreed as he didn't want dysentery to spread through the camp and my Granny was somehow contacted.

Granny and my uncle travelled down to Manila together, getting a lift from a local truck and a burro cart that was passing by. They returned to Baguio with Uncle Gary carrying me, and hitching a lift whenever they could. I was desperately sick so Granny took me to the nuns at the hospital. They took tremendous care of me, and although they had little medications, they eventually cured me - to my family's relief and delight.

When I was well enough to join them in their cave, Granny showed me how to dig for yams. At aged four my cousin Izzy and I would go out to forage for food. Coffee was also grown in the hills and we were taught how to look for the red beans, which were edible.

We instinctively kept a lookout for Japanese soldiers and as soon as we heard any we dived into bushes. I don't think they were interested in us as small children - there were so many waifs in the hills.

One day we met a nun from the convent and she gave me a small bantam egg. This was so precious. We had never had anything like it before. I held it carefully in my hand, close to my chest, and excitedly ran down the track to give it to Granny. We didn't have shoes - we were always barefoot - and I tripped over a tree root and fell flat on my face. I opened my hand and saw I had squashed the egg, but clutching it to me and howling my eyes out, I ran to Granny. I felt so guilty. Granny said not to worry and we could still eat it. So we sat for ages while she picked out fragments of shell and we ate the remains of the egg.

American fighter planes began flying over, which cheered us, recalled Diana. *One day one was shot down and a parachute opened. The area was very mountainous and there was a steep valley below us. The Japanese wanted to capture the pilot to get information from him but couldn't find him. After searching for him for a week they began to build a fence around the valley. They had decided to divide it and set fire to one half. If they didn't find the pilot they would torch the other half. There were a lot of people hiding in the jungle and we were among them.*

We watched one half going up in flames and knew we had to cross to the other side of the valley to be safe. The Japanese had orders to shoot anything that moved in the valley. There was a gate in the middle of the fence with a guard on it. We watched to find out when the guards changed and decided the best time to go was about three in the morning.

We hid in the bushes and waited for the guard change. Granny said she would go and speak to the guard as she was old, it was less likely they would shoot her, as Japanese had respect for older people. She also spoke some Japanese.

When Granny approached, the young guard challenged her and she replied in Japanese, "Don't shoot, I am an old lady." She told him she was with her family and three small children and wanted to get across to the hills to the other side of the valley in order to be safe.

The guard was surprised to hear her speaking Japanese and asked where she had learned it. It turned out he came from the same area where she had lived and his cousin had worked as a gardener for our family. He then said if he let her through he would be shot. Granny replied if we were caught we would say we had crawled under the fence and would say nothing about him. He said then go now, and told us which direction to take. We walked carefully around the camp, hoping not to disturb anyone, and into the jungle on the other side.

The next day the other side of the valley was set on fire and our cave was burned out completely. But still they never found the fighter pilot.

....

Java

Japan continued its sweeping attack on the South Pacific. Guam and the Wake islands were bombed; Siam (Thailand), Malaya, the Gilbert islands, Burma and Borneo were all invaded. Everywhere fell as quickly to the Japanese in the Far East as the countries in Europe had collapsed before Hitler. The Japanese were succeeding in dominating the area, and could now claim they were creating what they termed as their Co-Prosperity Sphere. But the prize they coveted most of all was Java, in the Dutch East Indies.

When Japan invaded the South Pacific, many fleeing the Phillipines, Singapore and Malaya tried to reach Java in the belief they would be safe in a Dutch colony. But for the Japanese, Java, with its huge stocks of oil, was their main target - the jewel in their new crown.

The motley remains of the British, Dutch, Australian and US navies struggled to resist the Japanese invasion on Java. But with virtually no air power the ships stood no chance against the bombing raids and submarine attacks launched by the new and more powerful Japanese navy.

On land the Dutch troops fought with courage but were hopelessly outnumbered. On 9 March 1942, three months after Pearl Harbour, the Dutch formerly surrendered Java.

Birgit Carolin, a Dutch girl living with her family in Java at that time, recalls her experience:

World War II had a decisive and permanently dislocating impact on my family, in common with millions of others; but we were very fortunate, emerging unscathed, unlike millions the world over. At the outbreak of war in Europe, we were living in Indonesia (then the Netherlands' East Indies) where my father was manager of a Dutch shipping line.

In 1941 my father was invited by the Dutch government, which was by then in exile in London, to fly out in order to assist in the war effort. At first he refused (my mother was about to give birth to their third daughter) suggesting an older colleague might go instead. The colleague refused to go, on the grounds that it would be madness to leave the safety of a stable Dutch colony far from hostilities!

Eventually, after my sister's birth and the attack on Pearl Harbour, my father agreed to go, but he insisted that he be allowed to travel with his family to Australia, where my parents felt we would be safer. How wise they were - as later events proved!

When it became necessary for us to leave Java, just after Christmas 1941, I remember how our parents were at pains to explain why there would be no tree and no presents that year. It was always their principle to answer our questions as honestly as possible and to keep us informed of all they felt we needed to know. For me that policy worked: I trusted they would see to our safety. I cannot speak for my older sister, who tended to be much more anxious and apprehensive, always expecting the worst. Being older, she understood more of the dangers we were facing.

None of us knew when we left, that we would never return to live again in Indonesia – we took with us only one suitcase each. No room for my teddy bear, or our dog, Maidie, who had just had a litter of puppies. I grieved for the loss of these creatures, my dear and constant companions; also for Selma, our 'baboe' (Indonesian nanny), whose gentle care had ensured my sense of security, even more intimately than my mother's.

Looking back, I remember the confusion and bewilderment that I felt at the time; only now do I recognise the enormous loss occasioned by our abrupt departure from all that had constituted my small world. Plunged into the unknown, although surrounded by my family, I faced for the first time in my five years, the huge and terrifying world of strangers.

We flew to Sydney on 31st December 1941. I have an enduring nightmare vision of our New Year's Eve arrival in Sydney, where we were transported by taxi at midnight from the airport. Seen by my uncomprehending eyes through the windows of our taxi were huge faces, grotesquely leering, hectic activity, deafening noise and great white-skinned giants carousing too close for comfort. I was paralysed with fear and clung to my parents in panic.

As Birgit's father feared, it wasn't long before the Japanese attacked Australia. Darwin, in the Northern Territories had been extensively bombed and two Japanese submarines were captured in Sydney Harbour. The Dutch Government, in exile in London, were still keen for her father to help with the war effort. In spite of the dangers in the Pacific waters, he took the decision to travel to the United States with his family, where he would be closer to London. Birgit continues with her story:

After the Japanese invasion of the Indies in February 1942, we set sail on the SS President Grant, *a US merchant ship with a shanghaied crew of motley Filipino mariners. According to my father, we very nearly collided with the coast of New Zealand ('A miss is as a good as a mile', was the jovial captain's comment!), where a crowd of young airmen joined the ship.*

The ship was 'blacked out', sailing a southerly course to the west coast of South America, in order to avoid the Japanese submarines which succeeded in sinking both the ships before and after ours travelling the Pacific route.

My sister remembers being told after the war, that the option to travel together on a neutral Swedish ship was rejected by my parents, who preferred to risk being torpedoed by the enemy than being intercepted and separated by the Japanese, whose reputation for ruthlessness was well known. In Java, women and children were being interned, separated from men and boys over 12 years.

With each day that followed without incident, I felt more secure: life at sea was a familiar and reassuring experience. With many other children aboard, my sister Louise and I played happily on deck. Watching the New Zealander Air Force exercising each morning was intriguing: they were young, boisterous and funny. But at some level I must have been aware that danger lurked, because I have a clear memory of waking one morning to see a colourful view of Valparaiso (a port city on Chile's coast) framed in the port-hole, and feeling a rush of relief: a safe haven at last!

In March 1942, we reached California, and disembarked in San Francisco, later moving to New York. Days later Java capitulated to the Japanese. From then on, the threat for us receeded, although for my father it did not. He was constantly on the move in the USA, and in Canada and Britain. A gifted businessman and organiser, he worked on behalf of the Netherlands Government-in-Exile, and also worked tirelessly throughout the war for the British Ministry of War Transport and the American War Shipping Administration. His travels took him to perilous places – he was in London during the Blitz.

Whenever we said goodbye to him (as we frequently did during those war years) we had no idea whether he would return. I once found my sister in tears under the piano, weeping at the thought that we might never see our father again, and indignant that I was not upset too.

I could more easily accept his comings and goings and always trusted he would return – which he, fortunately, always did.

His work for the American War Shipping Administration involved the conversion of merchant vessels for hospital and troop use; to commission the construction of Liberty and victory ships and to oversee the Atlantic convoys. It was exhilarating work for him; he was making a significant contribution to the war effort and ultimately to the allied victory.

For my mother, the war years must have been very testing: there was palpable tension ever-present in the air. Anxious about my father, worried about her own parents, her brothers and friends in Europe and elsewhere, she was also cast upon her own resources in a strange country, raising three young children and managing a household with minimal help. Her pre-war life of leisure and luxury had not prepared her for this way of life. I remember her eccentric cooking and her insistence that we eat every morsel of our rationed food 'because other children everywhere are starving'. My sister and I belonged to The Clean Plate Club and wore our badges with pride.

I also remember my mother's incredible resilience, her determination to enjoy all that New York offered and to introduce us to its many pleasures. Full of vitality herself, she responded to the energy of this huge continent and its warm-hearted people.

....

Joan Diamantis and her family were also living in Java but they were unable to leave before the invasion and were imprisoned by the Japanese:

My parents were English missionaries and we lived a happy life with my older brother Peter in Bandung, Java, where I was born. Situated on a plateau surrounded by mountains, Bandung was very beautiful.

When I was 10 years old I was aware of the European war, particularly anything to do with Holland but also Norway as my best friend Ella was Norwegian. We used to meet every afternoon after siesta and draw in our books anything concerning daily life - mainly about school.

The school was Dutch and we sang patriotic songs and carried orange flags. At home my parents listened to the radio and news bulletins from the BBC, broadcast from London, which is how we heard about the sinking of the HMS Prince of Wales in Singapore.

With the Japanese advance I recall the anxiety of the adults. Daily routine began to be disrupted. Trenches were dug, air raid shelters built and the schools closed. Bandung was full of Allied troops and refugees. I no longer saw Ella.

My parents looked after troops and refugees who spoke of chaos with people milling about, many trying to escape. We children no longer played outside as there was talk of invasion. This became a reality when one day we heard a far-off humming noise. Japanese aircraft were bombing the town centre.

We rushed to the shelter, along with our Javanese servants, each with a small cloth bag containing our name, a whistle and chewing gum. I insisted on bringing my drawing books. Through a slit in the shelter we watched Dutch airplanes trying to defend the area and saw planes explode and debris, like matchsticks, floating down. This lasted only a few days. Apparently the Dutch forces had been sent elsewhere to support the Allies and Java and other islands were more or less left undefended.

The Japanese took over in March 1942 and my first sight of the army was when they arrived outside our house with bicycles, and several wristwatches on their arms, about to occupy a school now empty of Dutch troops. By now our house was boarded up and we had withdrawn to the back, living on dwindling food supplies. The Japanese took control. We had to put out Japanese flags and listening to foreign broadcasts became a punishable offence.

After about a month my parents were woken at night by loud banging and shouting. It transpired that my father had registered us at an address to which we were planning to move. The soldiers, on not finding him there, took a Scandinavian woman hostage. My father was then taken away to join other British prisoners and the hostage was released. We moved to the bigger place, which also housed other people, but our lives became more restricted.

Seven months later we were ordered to report to a school, Kleine Loekong, with instructions to bring a suitcase and mattress. My brother Peter, who was 14, was instantly put on a lorry and sent to prison. Luckily it was the same prison that my father was in, but we didn't know that at the time.

The school was made of plaited bamboo, which harboured bugs and other vermin. Although it was a British camp there were many other nationalities interned. In Malay, which was now the official language instead of Dutch, we were told that it was for our own protection that we were in the camp. We each only had space of a mat or mattress. These were to be rolled up during the day and it was forbidden to sit on them. Food was cooked on open fires. There was never enough wood and those who were brave enough stole more from an overlooked pile.

We were taught to come to the command Atsumari *(assemble),* Kioski *(stand to attention)* Kiri *(bow) and* Nori *(stand at ease). The first indication that the authorities meant business was when a tall woman was beaten because she showed lack of respect to a female Javanese warder. There were constant searches for contraband, jewellery, money, flags, etc.*

My education was fitful. I remember being taught to write a letter in English. That was about it. There were some girls I played with and also an impromptu concert by a Scottish professional singer with a beautiful voice.

In September 1943, at two o'clock in the morning, we were taken in buses to a railway station. We could take only a few clothes with us. I saw a large group of Chinese male prisoners crouching on the platform. It was cold and the place barely lit. We joined a train full of prisoners from elsewhere. Afterwards we heard stories of horrendous journeys taking days.

We were crowded into a sort of cattle truck. The windows were shuttered and there was no room to sit. As the day grew hot we needed water but there was none. Nearing the end of our journey the train stopped and the local railway guards gave us what water they could. It was only a sip each, but welcome.

We must have arrived some time in the night or early morning. We were put into open trucks and stood swaying until we reached a proper prison, Tanah Tinggi. We spent ages marching round and round the Japanese officers, our bits and pieces on the ground. Only after having our identities checked could we collect our stuff. Unfortunately my little drawing books were confiscated.

For a few weeks we lived in a very large room which resembled a market. In fact the women called it the fish market, because of its size and smell. Each person had a space to sleep on a long bench. There was a hole at one end surrounded by a low wall. This was the lavatory when we were locked in at night.

After some time women with children were allotted cells and my mother and I were locked in one of these at night.

Each day the flag was raised in the morning and lowered at night and the Japanese anthem sung by the soldiers accompanied by a trumpet. It seemed a rather sad tune to me. We had occasional searches and were shouted at, and we stood in the sun for hours. No hats, banana leaves or any head covering was allowed. If any high-ranking officer visited we had to face the walls. As usual daily life was boring and tedious and we were hungry.

After six months there we all had to walk, including the sick and old, with our parcels to the next camp, which was at an isolated spot called Tanerang. I remember those who were slow being shouted at to hurry. The Japanese commandant at the camp had a more liberal attitude towards entertainment. He allowed the famous Hungarian concert pianist, Lilly Kraus, to give a recital. A piano arrived and she played for us all, including the commandant and senior officers. There was also a show with singing and dancing. But other than this light relief, life was hard.

After the usual counting and searching through luggage had taken place, we found two spaces on a top bunk with several others. It was better than being on the bottom bunk. There were high and heavily barred windows but at least we had air even though it smelled of pig manure. Every night we were plagued by bugs and also rats running along the ceiling beams - though there was netting to stop them falling. There were gekkos too but they were nice and I loved watching them.

We had no soap or any cleaning materials. Again the loos were communal, as well as the showers.

Our diet was basically a sort of completely tasteless tapioca (without seasoning or sugar), a handful of rice and a piece of so-called bread which was about 2x4 inches big that was dark brown and very solid. We had vegetable soup with a bone or two and sometimes a really horrible offal paste was added (no heart, kidneys or liver). I had to sweep the kitchens and carry the waste in large baskets on a pole with some older woman to a dump just outside. Once I failed to see the guard and bow. He shouted and screamed at me but the older woman somehow persuaded him to do nothing.

We were there for three months before being sent by train to the next camp at Tjideng, Batavia (now Jakarta). Measles had broken out and I travelled in similar conditions as last time, but with a high fever. The camp was a compound of streets with large and small houses surrounded by two high bamboo walls and barbed wire. We had the usual waiting and standing - only this time I was ill and feverish.

Finally we were free to find a place. The Dutch women there were welcoming. I was put in a 'hospital' with no equipment or medicines but there were doctors and nurses. My mother had to find somewhere for us to sleep. There was no organising and it was always a matter of squeezing in more people.

The camp commandant was called Sonei. Apart from the twice daily roll call, he would call us out at night, usually at new moon. He would shout and hector us and hit the nearest woman.

We never knew what was going to happen. We all had a number to wear. This unpredictable regime was exhausting. He also fenced off houses from time to time and people were ordered to squash in with the rest. This happened to my mother and me but luckily we found a small verandah.

After the confinement of the other camps we liked the tree-lined streets. However the overcrowding meant that the cess-pits in the gardens of the houses overflowed into drains in front and the pit had to be cleared. Matters got worse as more people were crammed in. There were several thousand people packed into this camp.

My job was in a sewing room. There were five women sewing, mending, washing and ironing the clothes of the officers. I had to take the clean linen through two side gates to a bungalow, bow at the foot of some steps and hand it over to an orderly on a verandah.

One day I saw the commandant who called me onto the verandah. From his big chair and through an interpreter he asked why I was barefoot - and did I not know my feet would spread. He then told me to follow him to another verandah, took a couple of bananas from the top of a fridge and gave them to me. Not only was I very frightened but my fear was increased because I had to hide the fruit in my blouse, so that none of the prisoners would see them, and find my mother. We neither of us enjoyed eating them.

About this time we received a card from my brother written in Malay. We now knew he was alive.

Food became increasingly scarce and more people died. Dysentery was common and so was beri-beri. Sonei became increasingly erratic. The comandant punished us all because, he said, of smuggling. One day our daily bread lorry entered as usual, was unloaded then re-loaded and driven away. Next the rice and soup drums were emptied onto the ground. The women had to dig trenches, throw the food in and then cover it up. There was no food for three days.

Another portion of the camp was closed off and the women spokesmen had their hair shaved off and were mistreated. However, next day at roll call they turned up with turbans with curls of hair pinned to them. Conditions deteriorated and at one point we only had the tasteless tapioca, or something like it, to eat. It looked liked a colourless jelly and there was a lot of it but we could not eat much of it as it was so horrible. The days were mostly dreary. No music, no lessons, no reading. There were quarrels and fights.

Children of the Second World War

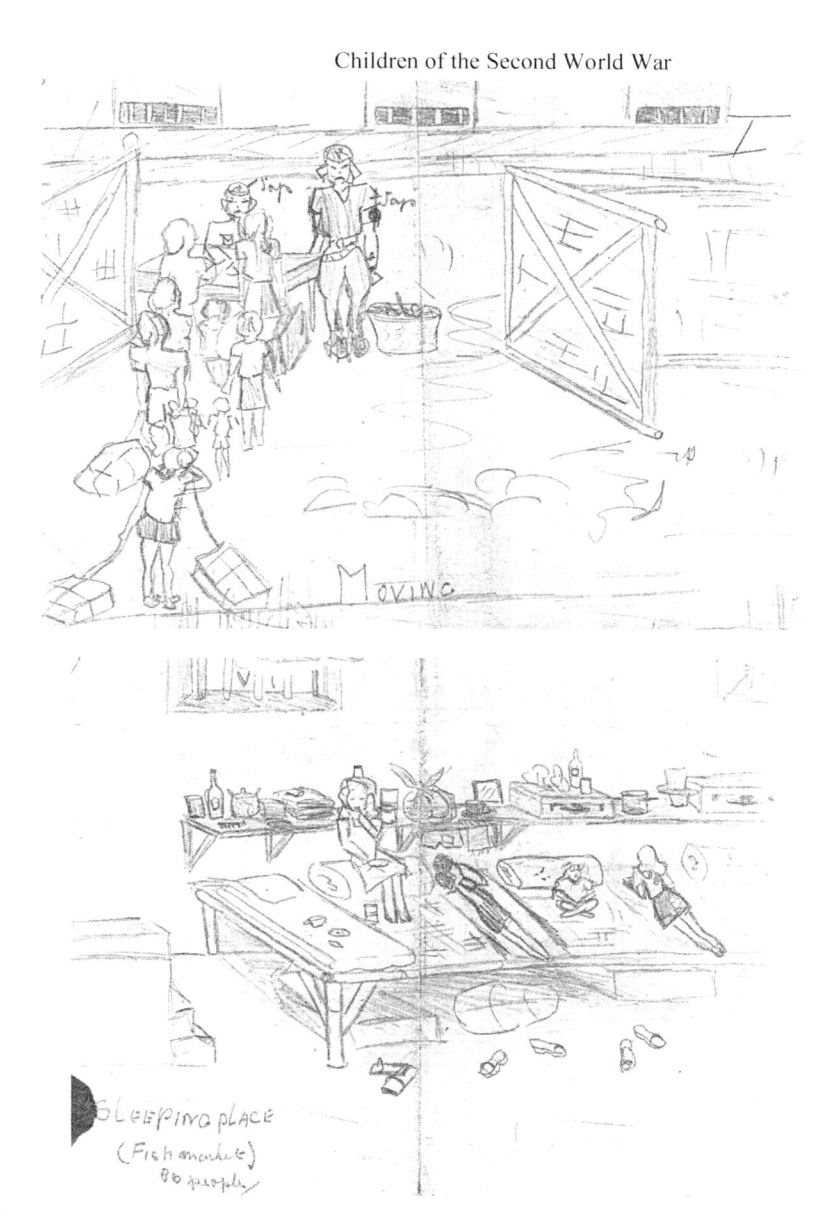

Sketches drawn by Joan Diamantis, age 12, while in a prisoner of war camp in Java during WW2

....

Shanghai: China

Corrinne Bottomley, who was born and brought up in Shanghai in China, remembers her early life there.

Before being interned, we had been living in a lovely street in the French Concession area called Rue Moliere, where Sun Yat-sen, founder of the Kuomintang (Nationalist Party), had once lived.

My father, Jack Ellery, had come to Shanghai from London in 1922 at the age of 20 to work as a prison officer at Ward Road Gaol. My mother, Sophie Sokoloff, was Russian and had grown up in Belorussia. Her older brother had been an officer in the Tsar's army and fled to Shanghai on the defeat of the White Russian Army. He became an architect with the municipal council and when my mother, at the age of 17, arrived in Shanghai, he obtained an introduction for her to the head of the Shanghai Waterworks and she became governess to his two children.

Although she hardly spoke a word of English at that time, she loved her work and the family and stayed with them until she met my father and married him in 1929. My sister was born a year later and I appeared on the scene in 1934.

War broke out between China and Japan in 1937 and Shanghai was severely bombed. My father sent my mother, my sister and myself to the safety of Hong Kong where we stayed for several months before returning.

When we were old enough, my sister and I attended a French-Canadian convent school called the Sacred Heart in Avenue Joffre, and every day we travelled to school by private rickshaw. Even when the Japanese invaded Shanghai again in December 1941, we continued to live in our house and go to school.

Two years later, in 1943, everything changed. My parents, my sister and I were put into a prisoner of war camp in Shanghai. I was nine years old at the time. There were 12 or 13 camps scattered around the city and ours contained about 800 people in quite a large area encompassing three former expatriate schools. We had ample playing fields and the classrooms were divided with partitions to make two or three living spaces. We were fortunate to have a sink with taps and running water in ours, and a window, which looked out over a compound onto a main road.

Every morning we had to stand outside the door to our room to be inspected by the guard, who would come into the room to check if we were too ill to get up. We slept on camp beds and, in winter, we would wear our pajamas beneath our clothes to keep out the cold.

There was an assortment of teachers in the camp who taught the subjects they knew best, which is why I learned Latin at such a young age. The teachers were mostly very good – but hungry and bad-tempered. There were exercise books at first, and a few library books, pencils and chalk, and we sat on long benches at long tables in front of blackboards. Towards the end of our imprisonment, when paper was scarce, we had to write on very flimsy sheets of Japanese toilet paper.

Food was prepared and meted out by the male inmates. It chiefly consisted of red stony rice, baby octopus, cuttlefish, buffalo meat, Japanese misouami (honey) and brown bread. We now know the red rice and brown bread must have been quite nutritious, but we didn't appreciate it at the time.

There was a system of bartering for clothing as no one had money. I remember having to wear purple suede high heels for a while - quite unsuitable for a child – and I hurt my foot badly in a fall when wearing them. There was a clinic for minor ailments, but for serious medical conditions, we were taken to a proper hospital. I was in one for three weeks after an appendectomy.

My mother's brother, being Russian, was not interned. Once he tried to sneak an electric iron over the fence to my mother. This was intercepted by Japanese guards and so mother had to face their wrath and was kept in the guardhouse for several hours enduring verbal abuse - but nothing worse, thank goodness.

Another time I was playing with a mirror at the window in our room, unaware it was reflecting the sun and flashing into one of the shops. The shopkeeper reported it so we were then confronted by an angry Japanese guard accusing my father of trying to send secret messages.

Parents all took turns to perform various tasks. My father stoked fires in the kitchen, mended shoes with old bicycle tyres and swept floors. My mother cooked and sewed and made toys from the food parcel boxes we received from "outside". These contained scrumptious things like Hershey chocolate bars, Rose Mill pate, Kraft cheese and condensed milk from American G.I. rations.

One inmate was actually assisted in setting up a form of factory making soya bean milk - which was truly delicious and which I love to this day. One of the children's "duties" was to deliver the milk from door to door.

We made our own entertainment. There were some talented and enthusiastic people who put on plays and musical evenings, which seemed to please the Japanese guards sitting in the front row. I learned *to tap dance and do ballet - and also roller skate, if that can be called 'entertainment'. We children played a form of hockey, cricket and softball, and the bachelor men played a good deal of baseball.*

****

CHAPTER EIGHT
JAPAN SURRENDERS: WAR ENDS

Kensuke Fukae was a schoolboy in Tokyo, Japan, during the Second World War but in later years he emigrated to the United States where he became Vice President of Minolta for 25 years before starting his own company Kentek Information Systems in Allendale, New Jersey.

Kensuke hailed from a high-status samurai family and, before the war, lived a wealthy life going to the best schools. But the war left the entire Japanese population suffering terribly with nearly 75 percent at starvation level and nearly everyone reduced to poverty. Kensuke spoke of having to eat plaster from the walls and bits of grass to stave off hunger pangs. Japanese families lost businesses, property, friends and family in the firebombing, and yet they bowed down to the propaganda of the Japanese war machine. Kensuke wrote an opinion piece about his experience of the war in *The New York Times* in 1985. His daughter, Amy Massey, kindly gave her permission for it to be reproduced in this book.

At school on the morning of December 8, 1941, the battle station bell of the flagship Mikasa pealed out, as it did every morning, for roll-call. The Mikasa had led the Japanese victory over the Russian Baltic fleet; the bell was yet one more daily reminder of the Japanese military traditions that my schoolmates and I lived to uphold. But that morning the bell had another resonance: at breakfast, my mother and brother and I had heard the news of our attack on Pearl Harbor.

As junior high school students, we had learned that our virtual annexation of Manchuria was our protection against the advance of Communism after a power vacuum was created by the collapse of the Chin dynasty. It was also true, however, that the Depression had resulted in the collapse of Japan's Western markets, and the population had doubled in 50 years. Expansion through military conquest seemed to be a solution to many of Japan's economic problems.

The Japanese group mentality and the "samurai" spirit strengthened the cause of those who urged military spending and strength. Our traditions, after all, taught us not to question leadership and authority. Anyone who questioned the military budget was considered "hikoku-min," or "non-citizen," and as such was thought to be endangering our sacred national security. The more aggressive the military became, the more it was able to win concessions from the moderate elements in the government who feared being condemned as un-Japanese.

The United States reacted to the occupation of points in Indochina by declaring a virtual trade embargo that included oil. On December 8, we were told that our strike was against a hostile nation that was usurping Japanese property, choking off oil, and demanding our withdrawal from China. In the schoolyard, talk was excited and patriotic. We were 16; in a short time, more than a third of us would take our places in the army and naval academies. Not long after that, school was, practically speaking, suspended, as the entire nation was mobilised for military training or industry.

Along with the virtual annexation of Manchuria in 1933 came the establishment of an actual "Thought Police." The military establishment now controlled not only the administration, but also the media. Censorship of news was sanctioned for "national security reasons." Anyone - be they editor, professor or politician - expressing a dissenting opinion could be arrested as a Communist sympathiser or similar undesirable. Patriotism ran high in our isolated land, and the administration defined all of its actions in terms of national security.

Within a few years, the media was being used to exhort the people to fight to the glorious end. The kamikaze mentality flourished as citizens of all ages literally sharpened bamboo spears to ward off invaders. Firebombs rained destruction on every major city except the old capital,

Kyoto. On March 10, 1945, 200 B-29 bombers incinerated more than 50 percent of metropolitan Tokyo and 80,000 residents. On August 6 and 9, the United States dropped atomic bombs on Hiroshima and Nagasaki, respectively.

On August 14, we were told that a very important announcement would be made the next day. On August 15, 1945, Emperor Hirohito of Japan was heard on the radio for the first time announcing that the Japanese government had accepted the Potsdam Declaration which demanded the unconditional surrender of the Japanese military. For over 2000 years the Emperor had been regarded as the sacred descendant of the Shinto God. None of us had ever heard his voice. We accepted that the war was over, though we were still ready to die for our country. It was a moment of relief and disappointment; almost everybody cried.

In the next several days, many officers committed hara-kiri, in keeping with the samurai code. Some young men organised partisan groups to fight to the death rather than be held captive. But for most of us, the Emperor's order was absolute. We were and are a deeply patriotic nation.

America, unlike Japan, has a strong tradition of dissent. This country was built on the right to challenge authority. Such a tradition was tragically absent in my homeland as I grew up; Americans should cherish it, for it is such rights that most merit their patriotic devotion. Our loyalty was to our leaders - America's must be to the Constitution.

****

8th June, 1946

TO-DAY, AS WE CELEBRATE VICTORY, I send this personal message to you and all other boys and girls at school. For you have shared in the hardships and dangers of a total war and you have shared no less in the triumph of the Allied Nations.

I know you will always feel proud to belong to a country which was capable of such supreme effort; proud, too, of parents and elder brothers and sisters who by their courage, endurance and enterprise brought victory. May these qualities be yours as you grow up and join in the common effort to establish among the nations of the world unity and peace.

George R.I.

A letter sent to school children who lived through WW2 from King George VI

ABOUT THE AUTHOR

Helen Massey (Née Bendall) was born in Hong Kong and evacuated to Australia with her mother and three brothers during the Second World War. Her story is documented in this book along with the stories of other people she had connections with both in the Far East and in Europe.

Helen returned to Hong Kong after the war and later settled in the UK where she worked as a journalist and sub-editor for womens' magazines. She met Patrick Massey, then working for the Associated Press, on Fleet Street in London and they married and had two children, Bryan and Shauna. The WW2 memories of Patrick, who died in 2009, are also documented in this book. Sadly, after a short illness, Helen died in 2012 before she could finish *Children of the Second World War*.

Although being a refugee in Australia was a difficult time in Helen's life, she also had many happy memories of her time there. It was her wish to have her ashes scattered in the place where she used to play as a child refugee in Sydney.